Walleye Secrets

MINNETONKA, MINNESOTA

In this book, author Dick Sternberg combines biological expertise with angling savvy to present a unique, in-depth perspective on the sport of walleye fishing.

Walleye Secrets

Printed in 2013.

Laura Hunter
Vice President Product Marketing

Jen Weaverling
Managing Editor

Jenny Mahoney
Book Design and Production

Bill Lindner Photography (Bill Lindner, Tom Heck, Brook Martin, Jason Lund, Pete Cozad, Dare Devil Diver and Mark Emery)
Dick Sternberg
Animals Animals / ©Carol Geake, p.147
Animals Animals / ©C. Milins-OSF, p.147
Animals Animals / ©Donald Specker, p.147
Photography

Dave Schelitzche
Joe Tomelleri, pp.24 (2), 26, 29
Clarinda Color Art Department, p.110
Lakemaps™, p.138
Sportman's Connection, pp.113, 148 (2), 155
Illustration

Special Thanks: Shawn Bjonfald, Tom Carpenter, Julie Cisler, Gina Germ, Ryan Gilligan, Dave Schelitzche and Michelle Teigen.

3 4 5 6 7 8 9 10 / 18 17 16 15 14 13
ISBN: 978-1-58159-475-1
©2011 North American Fishing Club

North American Fishing Club
12301 Whitewater Drive
Minnetonka, MN 55343
www.fishingclub.com

CONTENTS

INTRODUCTION

If there was ever a man who lived and breathed walleye fishing, it's Dick Sternberg.

Dick has been fishing ol' marble 'eyes for decades, and in the process has fished virtually every type of water in which walleyes are found. He is truly an expert's expert.

Walleye Secrets is the result of Dick's lifetime pursuit of walleye and walleye fishing knowledge. He relies heavily on his training and field work as a fisheries biologist, as well as his extensive on-the-water experience as an angler.

The walleye, more than just about any other fish, has long been surrounded by an air of mystery. *Walleye Secrets* breaks through the mysteries and shreds misconceptions that have plagued walleye anglers for years.

In the following pages, you will learn more about the walleye, the waters in which it lives, and the tackle and techniques that produce, than you would spending years on the water.

Yes, *Walleye Secrets* is that good!

WALLEYE BASICS

The first step to improving your walleye-fishing success is to remove the aura of mystery surrounding these elusive gamefish.

What You Need to Know About Walleyes

I once caught the biggest walleye in the "Governor's Fishing Opener," an annual event sponsored by the Minnesota Department of Tourism. But when it came time to award the prize, the organizers declared that I wasn't eligible. As a fisheries biologist who worked on the same waters we were fishing, I had an "unfair advantage," they said.

In that particular case, a good jig-fishing touch had a lot more to do with my catching the fish than my biology background. But there's no doubt that a general understanding of walleye behavior and the factors that influence it will go a long way toward putting more fish into your boat.

Here are the most important things you need to know about walleyes:

Vision

Walleyes differ from most other freshwater fish in that the retina of their eye has one of nature's amazing inventions—the tapetum lucidum—which is a layer of reflective pigment that intensifies any light the retina receives. As a result, walleyes can see very well in dimly-lit waters where most other fish cannot, giving them a distinct advantage over most prey species, such as yellow perch.

Many nocturnal animals, such as raccoons, opossums and cats, also have a tapetum, explaining why their eyes glow when struck by light. We've all seen the shining eyes of a house cat in a ditch as we've driven along a dark road at night; a walleye's eyes shine in the same manner when a light strikes them.

Walleyes seldom feed in brightly-lit water. It's not so much that the bright light "hurts their eyes," as we often hear; it's just that they would have no

predatory edge over their prey under those conditions.

How much light penetrates to the fish depends mainly on water clarity. Here's a simple clarity test that will give you an idea of when walleyes are most likely to feed, and when you're most likely to catch them. On a bright, calm day, tie a white jig to your line and lower it into the water. If it disappears in the first three feet, do your fishing during the day. If it vanishes between three and eight feet, schedule your fishing around dawn and dusk. If you can see the jig beyond eight feet, you'll probably do best at night. Of course, weather conditions (p.12) can greatly alter this feeding schedule.

The angle at which light rays strike the water determines how much of the light will penetrate to the depths and how much will be reflected. In summer, when the midday sun is high in the sky, the light beats straight down on the water, penetrating deeply and keeping walleyes out of the shallows in daylight hours. In spring and fall, when the sun is at a much lower angle, a high percentage of the sunlight is reflected, so walleyes often remain in the shallows all day.

Canadian fisheries researchers found that walleyes in a clear lake bit best just when the sun was disappearing below the horizon and the light intensity was rapidly decreasing. But a sudden decrease in light level seems to trigger walleyes most anytime. When the dark clouds preceding a thunderstorm roll in, for instance, walleyes usually go on a feeding rampage.

A sudden decrease in light intensity usually triggers a walleye feeding spree.

Color vision tests conducted on walleyes measured how strongly their eyes reacted to various colors in the spectrum. The longer the horizontal color bar, the stronger the reaction to that color.

You can still catch walleyes in near-freezing water, but it takes a slow presentation.

Walleyes can definitely see color, but their color vision is weakest in the blue-violet range of the spectrum and strongest in the orange-red to yellow-green portion.

Although the color chart above seems to correlate fairly well with what we normally consider good walleye colors, I wouldn't

recommend using it as a color-selection guide. Water color and depth also affect what a walleye sees and, in many cases, resemblance to natural forage is more important than color. The best way to find the right color is by trial and error.

Temperature Preferences

Biologists classify the walleye as a coolwater species, meaning that it has a preferred temperature range between that of warmwater fish like largemouth bass or catfish, and coldwater fish like trout or salmon. Walleyes favor water temperatures in the 55- to 75-degree range, with an optimal temperature of about 69.

At water temperatures below 50, the walleye's metabolism is slow. It requires little food and makes only short feeding movements. Because of its slow metabolism, food is digested gradually, so a meal lasts a long time. As a result, early-season walleye fishing is often a bust, especially in an unseasonably cold spring.

As the water temperature rises into the preferred range, the walleye's metabolism increases. It demands more food and must spend more time chasing prey. And the warming water speeds its digestion rate, so a meal doesn't last as long as it did earlier. This explains why walleye fishing improves when the water reaches the mid- to upper-50-degree range.

Walleye anglers know how tough fishing can be during the hottest part of the summer. Water temperatures above the walleye's preferred range can slow its activity, but only in rare instances is warm water the cause of the fishing slowdown. In all but the shallowest lakes, walleyes can escape the warm temperature simply by going deeper, assuming the depths have an adequate level of dissolved oxygen (about 4 parts per million). But why, then, is midsummer fishing often so poor? The answer will become apparent when we discuss food habits (p.10).

Fishing generally picks up again as the water cools in fall. The fish feed heavily to put on a layer of fat that will carry them through the winter and provide the nourishment needed for their developing eggs. But even though the fish are actively feeding, fishing gets tough once the fall turnover (p.150) begins. With the water at a uniform temperature from top to bottom, the fish may be at any depth, so finding them can be a problem.

Water temperature also determines when walleyes spawn, which, in turn, has a major effect on their feeding behavior (p.23).

Bottom Type

Given a choice, walleyes invariably select a hard bottom over a soft one. Bottom types most likely to hold walleyes include rubble, gravel, sand or a combination of these materials.

Walleyes are seldom found over silt or soft muck, probably because this type of bottom has little invertebrate life to attract baitfish. Also, loose silt would be sucked into the gills if a walleye were to rest on the bottom.

Food Habits

Like most other predatory gamefish, walleyes will eat whatever food nature provides. But the bulk of their diet consists of small fish. As a rule, walleyes prefer long, slim-bodied baitfish because they are easier to swallow than deep-bodied types. Food preferences will be covered more thoroughly on pages 22 to 31.

Populations of most types of forage fish fluctuate tremendously, greatly affecting the walleye's feeding patterns.

In many rivers and reservoirs, for instance, walleyes feed primarily on shad. Although large walleyes may eat a 1- or 2-year-old shad, most of those consumed are young-of-the-year. Shad and most other forage fish spawn in spring, so the young don't reach a size attractive to walleyes until midsummer.

Although warming water in spring increases the walleye's need for food, the number of eating-size shad that are available is at the annual low. The population of young shad from the previous year has been greatly reduced by predation, so the walleyes' hunger is not easily satisfied. Consequently, they spend a good deal of their time in search of food, explaining why walleye fishing is usually good in spring and early summer.

➤ Newly hatched shad are too small to appeal to adult walleyes, but by midsummer they've grown to an appetizing size. For the next month or so, walleyes lead the good life. With huge schools of shad virtually everywhere, walleyes can easily eat their fill in a few minutes. You'll hear fishermen say that the walleyes have stopped feeding but, in reality, the fish are consuming more food than at any other time of the year. However, unless you're lucky enough to be at the right place with the right bait during the short "bite," you're in for some lousy fishing.

But the good life usually doesn't last long. Young-of-the-year shad appeal not only to walleyes, but also to other predator fish like largemouth and smallmouth bass, so shad numbers quickly dwindle. By fall, shad are getting harder to find, so the walleyes must again resume their search for food. They move about more than they did in summer and their feeding periods are longer. In cases where the baitfish hatch is exceptionally large, however, poor fishing may persist through the winter and even into the next year.

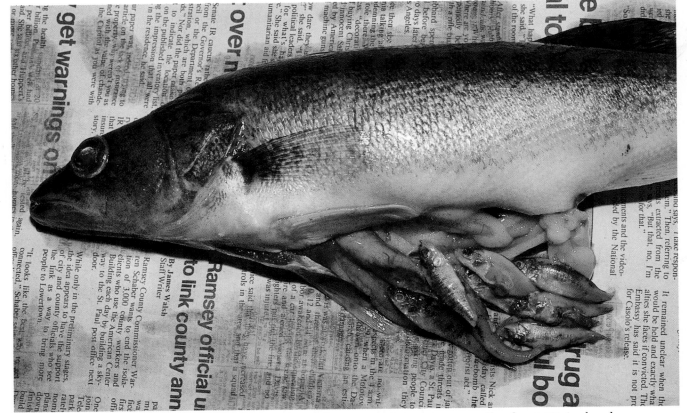

Walleyes go on a feeding rampage once perch reach an appetizing size, usually about 2½ inches long.

Perch, shiners and most other types of walleye forage also have annual cycles of abundance that greatly affect fishing.

A walleye's diet may change abruptly when a large supply of food suddenly becomes available. During a mayfly hatch, for example, walleyes may stop eating baitfish and switch entirely to mayfly nymphs. They continue to gorge themselves on the wriggling larvae as long as the hatch continues.

Growth

In waters where food is abundant, walleyes grow rapidly and reach trophy size quickly. In a reservoir with a large crop of shad, for example, a walleye may reach 10 pounds in only 7 years. But in a lake with a modest perch population, it may take twice as long to reach that size.

Latitude also has a major effect on growth rate. Because of the longer growing season, walleyes grow much faster in the South than in the North. But because of the warmer water, Southern walleyes "burn

A walleye's long, recurved teeth make it difficult for prey to escape.

out" much sooner. Their maximum life span is only about 8 years, versus 12 to 20 years in Northern waters. Consequently, Southern walleyes don't necessarily reach a larger size.

A fast-growing walleye (left) has a small head in comparison to the rest of its body. On a slow-growing walleye (right), the reverse is true.

Effects of Weather

I know a guy who won't go fishing until he checks the daily fish activity forecast to see when they're going to bite. Evidently, lots of people take these charts seriously. But there is one thing they're failing to consider: activity forecasts published months in advance can't factor in the effects of weather, and that is probably the most important variable in determining when walleyes feed.

I once tried checking one of these charts against my own fishing results for several weeks. I was surprised to find a strong correlation, but there was one problem—the correlation was negative. My fishing was worst at the times when the charts said it should be best. It was almost like the chart-maker was onto something, but he had his formula upside down.

For the best walleye fishing in waters of medium to high clarity, I like overcast skies and moderate winds, which create a choppy surface. These conditions reduce light intensity, prompting walleyes to feed longer in the morning and begin feeding earlier in the afternoon. But in low-clarity waters, these same conditions may slow the action because they reduce visibility too much.

The conditions I dread most are sunny days after a cold front and the days following a severe thunderstorm. Nobody really knows why walleyes shut off following the passage of a cold front; some speculate that it's a result of the ultraclear, haze-free skies, which allow more sunlight to penetrate the atmosphere and reach the lake surface. Scuba divers have told me of seeing cold-front walleyes lying flat to the bottom with their fins touching, and being able to swim up and touch them.

Good luck trying to catch those fish!

I'm convinced that loud thunderclaps affect walleyes in much the same way as cold fronts. The fish simply go dormant and refuse to bite. I was once fishing on a city lake on the 4th of July, just prior to the fireworks show. Despite all the boats milling around to get into position for a good view, the fish were biting. I had boated half a dozen walleyes and lost several more when the first rocket exploded overhead. The deafening explosion shook my boat, much like a lightning bolt hitting 10 feet away. The walleyes shut off like someone flipped a switch, and the same thing happens after loud thunderclaps. The more severe the thunder, the longer the fish stay dormant; bad storms may wipe out fishing for up to three days.

How Weather Affects Walleye Fishing

Overcast skies and a moderate chop limit light penetration in clear waters, so walleyes often bite most of the day.

Sunny skies and a relatively calm surface usually mean good walleye fishing in muddy waters.

Spawning Habits

In early spring, male walleyes begin to congregate around shoal areas and the mouths of inlet streams, usually when the water temperature reaches about 34 degrees. Although the fish are starting to feed more heavily, the "bite" is still sporadic.

Females remain scattered in deeper water until the water reaches 38 to 42 degrees, then they join the males and pre-spawn feeding starts in earnest. From now until the onset of spawning, anglers enjoy excellent walleye action, assuming the fishing season is open.

Spawning usually begins when the water reaches 46 to 48 degrees, but water temperature is not the sole factor determining when walleyes spawn.

Just as a hen has to incubate her eggs for about 21 days for them to hatch, walleye eggs also require a certain amount of heat in order to ripen. If the water temperature has been low and then rises rapidly because of a few warm days, the total heat requirement will not be met and walleyes will not spawn, even if the temperature reaches 50 degrees. If the water warms gradually, on the other hand, the total heat requirement may be met by the time the water reaches 44.

Walleyes are reluctant to bite once spawning begins, although I've seen females spewing eggs as they were boated, so spawners do bite occasionally. But once spawning is completed, females enter a recuperation period lasting 10 to 14 days. During this time, catching them is next to impossible. Luckily, all walleyes do not ripen at once. So even though

Anglers catch easy limits, mostly males, during the post-spawn feeding binge.

most fish are in the spawning or recuperation stage, a few are usually still "green" and willing to bite. And late in the spawning period, a few early spawners have already recuperated and are starting to feed. This means you can almost always catch a few fish by toughing it out.

Following the recuperation period, walleyes in most lakes school around 5- to 10-foot-deep sand-gravel shoal areas that offer an abundant supply of baitfish. Walleyes may feed in these areas throughout the day for two to three weeks to regain weight lost in spawning.

Even a novice can usually catch walleyes during the post-spawning feeding binge. On many waters, the bulk of the walleye catch for the entire year occurs during this period.

But most of this early post-spawn catch consists of male walleyes, which are generally smaller than females. Males do not require as much time to recuperate from the rigors of spawning, so they begin to bite before the females.

Some females start to feed about a week after the males, but the recuperation period for the biggest females lasts a little longer. Once they start to feed, however, your chances of catching a trophy walleye are better than at any other time of year (p.14).

As the guy who checks the fish activity forecasts every day is learning, there are no shortcuts to walleye fishing success. You can't rely on charts or hope to catch fish just because you have a tackle box bulging with all the latest baits. You must understand walleye behavior and all the factors that affect it, and then tailor your fishing plans accordingly.

"Big Time" for Walleyes

When the big females turn on several weeks after spawning, you've got a good chance to catch walleyes like this beauty.

In many states, the walleye season is closed during the spawning period but opens soon after spawning has been completed. Millions of anglers, eager to get in on the early-season bonanza, crowd every lake or river known to hold a walleye. The madness goes on for about two weeks, during which time some waters yield 50 percent or more of the walleyes they will produce for the entire year. Lots of anglers go home with a batch of nice "eaters," but surprisingly few really big walleyes are seen.

That's because practically all big walleyes are females, and with spawning only a few days behind them, they are still in a weakened condition and have not yet had time to recuperate enough to start feeding. They begin to feed a little a couple of weeks after spawning, but the major feeding binge starts much later, usually five to seven weeks after spawning. This is "big time" for serious trophy hunters.

Exactly when the big walleyes turn on varies, depending mainly on latitude and depth of the lake. For example, walleyes in the sandy, mid-depth lakes in central Minnesota spawn around April 22 in a normal spring. The year's very best trophy walleye fishing in these lakes begins about five weeks later, usually in early June.

In the deep, cold "shield" lakes of southern Canada, walleyes spawn up to two weeks later. Plus, these deep lakes take from 10 to 15 days longer to warm up than do the mid-depth lakes. So the feeding binge begins three to four weeks later, usually from late June to early July.

Knowledgeable anglers make it a point to hit the proven trophy walleye lakes during this peak period, and some of the most impressive walleye catches ever recorded have been taken then.

Here's the reason fishing for trophy-caliber walleyes is so good at this time. When the females finally

June 29 (55°N)

June 24 (52.5°N)

June 18 (50°N)

June 11 (47.5°N)

June 3 (45°N)

May 26 (42.5°N)

May 18 (40°N)

May 10 (37.5°N)

May 2 (35°N)

Big time for walleyes starts much earlier in the South than in the North. In northern Arkansas (latitude 35°N) for example, post-spawn action in a normal year peaks on about May 2. In southern Canada (latitude 50°N), the post-spawn action usually peaks around June 18.

recover from spawning, they have deeply sunken bellies, the result of not eating for nearly two months. They're desperately in need of food, but the supply of eating-size baitfish in the lake is at the annual low. The baitfish that hatched in spring are not yet large enough to eat, and the ones that hatched the previous spring have been largely depleted through predation. In order to satisfy their hunger, the walleyes have to stay more active and spend more of their time feeding than they normally would. But once their initial hunger is satisfied, feeding activity slows considerably. You'll have to work a lot harder for the fish, and the ones you catch will have a much chunkier look. The feeding peak lasts from one to three weeks, depending on the lake.

The best way that I know to get onto braggin'-size walleyes is to watch the online fishing reports around the time of the feeding peak. Try to get a feel for what lakes turn on at what times. If you see several big walleye listings for the same lake, note the lake name and when the fish were caught. By the time you see this information, however, the bite may be over. Nevertheless, file it away and use it to plan a trip for next year. If you're willing to do some legwork during the winter, you could check your files and the newspaper archives and put together a plan in time for the feeding binge.

If you're intent on catching a 10-pound-plus walleye, planning your trip during "big time" is the single most important thing you can do. In my experience, more than half of the trophy walleyes caught each year, including some in the 13- to 15-pound category, are taken during this short period. When you're fishing for walleyes of this size, however, there are no guarantees. There will be days when they hit practically anything you throw at them, but that's highly unusual. After all, if the fish were that stupid, they wouldn't be big.

Online fishing reports and forums can clue you into when specific lakes' trophy potential is peaking.

WALLEYE VS. SAUGER

I once read a story in a outdoors newspaper that advised readers that a certain river was producing good numbers of saugers and a few walleyes. That was a true statement. The writer then went on to say that if you wanted to catch walleyes, you'd have to fish 10 feet deeper than you would for saugers. With that statement, his credibility instantly evaporated, leading me to three possible conclusions:

- He had never fished for walleyes and saugers and didn't know any better.
- He was interviewing anglers that didn't have a clue.
- He meant that the saugers were 10 feet deeper than the walleyes.

In a lifetime of fishing waters that abound with walleyes and saugers, I've yet to see a time when the walleyes were deeper. As I'll explain later, there's a solid biological reason why this is the case. Even though walleyes and saugers are very close relatives, there are many biological differences that have important implications for anglers. Here are the most significant of those differences and some advice on tailoring your fishing methods accordingly:

Vision

Much has been written about the walleye's ability to see well in dim light. As already discussed (p.6), a walleye's retina has a layer of reflective pigment, called the *tapetum lucidum*, that intensifies any light the eye receives. The sauger's eye also has a *tapetum*, but it differs considerably from the walleye's in that it covers a much larger portion of the retina. Consequently, saugers can see even better than walleyes in dim light.

The sauger's dim-light vision may well be the best of any freshwater fish species. This explains why saugers invariably inhabit deeper water than walleyes. In my experience, they can be anywhere from 5 to 50 feet deeper.

North Dakota's giant Lake Sakakawea heads the list of the country's top sauger factories. In 1971, the lake yielded the world-record sauger, an 8 pound, 12 ouncer, and it is also known

A sauger's tapetum is even larger than a walleye's, which means the sauger sees even better in dim light.

for its trophy walleyes. I like to fish the lake in late fall, because the walleyes are feeding heavily on shallow, rocky points—usually at depths of 5 feet or less. The saugers also go on a feeding rampage in fall, but they're usually at depths of 30 feet or more and I've caught them as deep as 55.

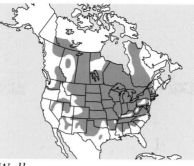

Walleye range.

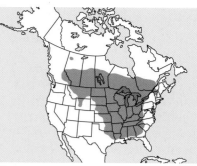

Sauger range.

Know the Difference

Walleyes and saugers belong to the perch family (*Percidae*) and are very closely related. Although the maximum size of saugers is less than half that of walleyes, they are highly desirable gamefish. In some waters, however, each species has a separate limit, so it's important to be able to distinguish between the two.

IGFA World Records:
Walleye—25 pounds, 0 ounces; Old Hickory Lake, Tennessee; August 2, 1960.
Sauger—8 pounds, 12 ounces; Lake Sakakawea, North Dakota; October 6, 1971.
Note: IGFA reinstated world record in 2010

Walleyes have golden sides and a white belly. The spiny dorsal fin is not spotted, but has a black blotch at the rear base. The lower lobe of the tail has a large, white tip.

Saugers are grayish to brownish with dark blotches. The dorsal fin has rows of distinct black spots, and the pectoral fins have a dark spot at the base. The lower lobe of the tail may have a thin white streak.

Water Clarity

The sauger's unique visual capability also explains why it thrives in murky water. In turbid lakes or rivers that hold both saugers and walleyes, saugers usually gain the upper hand, often outnumbering walleyes by as much as 15 to one. In clearer waters, the reverse is usually true. In a large bay of Ontario's giant Lake Nipigon, walleyes were the predominant species until turbid water was diverted into the bay. Within a few years, saugers greatly outnumbered walleyes.

Lakes fed by large rivers often have great fisheries for both walleyes and saugers. But don't expect top-rate angling for both in the same part of the lake. As a rule, saugers predominate in the upper reaches, where muddy river water keeps the clarity low. Walleyes are more numerous in the lower reaches, because the silt has had a chance to settle out and the water is clearer. In Lake Pepin, a widening of the Mississippi River along the Minnesota-Wisconsin border, saugers abound in the upper half of the lake, where the Mississippi dumps its silt load. But in the lower half, where the water is clearer and the bottom less silty, walleyes are the primary angling target.

Bottom Preference

Saugers are often referred to as "sand pike," a name that reflects their preference for a sandy bottom. In waters that have a mixture of rocky and sandy habitat, look for walleyes on the rocks and saugers on a sandy or even silty bottom. Another difference: Unlike walleyes, saugers are seldom found in the weeds. I doubt that they have an aversion to weedy cover; it's just that weeds seldom grow at the depths they normally inhabit.

Saugers also seem to be linked to the bottom more strongly than are walleyes. I have yet to see saugers suspend, while walleyes in many lakes suspend regularly to feed on ciscoes, shad or other pelagic (open water) baitfish.

Current Requirements

Saugers are fish of big rivers. Although they will tolerate stronger current than walleyes, they are typically found in slow-moving water. They sometimes inhabit lakes, but only those connected to big rivers. Walleyes, on the other hand, are equally at home in rivers and in lakes, even lakes with no river connection.

Migratory Habits

Tagging studies have shown that saugers are the most migratory member of the perch family. They have

Habitat Preferences—Walleye vs. Sauger

Saugers prefer a sandy bottom, explaining why they're often called "sand pike."

Walleyes are more likely to be found on a rocky or gravelly bottom, but they will also hold on firm sand.

been recovered as much as 236 miles from their point of release. In my own tagging studies on the Mississippi River, I also found saugers to be more migratory than walleyes. One sauger, tagged in the summer around Buffalo City, Wisconsin, was caught the following spring below the Taylor's Falls dam on the St. Croix River. To get there, the fish had to swim 65 miles up the Mississippi—passing through two navigation dams—and then continue 50 miles up the St. Croix.

Spawning Habits

In most waters, saugers begin to spawn about the time walleyes are finishing. If you go by water temperature, walleyes usually start spawning at about 48 degrees; saugers, about 52. Walleyes deposit their eggs in 1 to 6 feet of water; saugers, 4 to 12 feet. Although both species may spawn on the same rocky shoals, their depth preferences are different enough that there is little overlap.

Short strikes are common in sauger fishing.

Feeding Habits

Walleyes are known for their finicky feeding habits but, compared to saugers, they're super-aggressive, especially in cold water. At water temperatures below 45 degrees, saugers have a frustrating habit of sucking on the bait without swallowing it. If you're using a minnow, it will often come back with a ripped up tail. Cold-water walleyes are not above striking short, but with saugers it's almost a given.

Saugers can see well even where there is minimal light penetration, explaining why they're commonly caught in muddy or deep water.

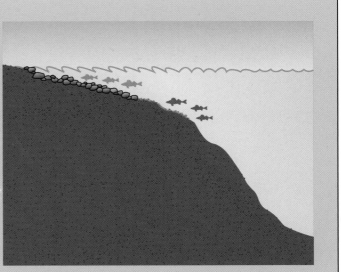

Saugers (blue) and walleyes (red) may spawn on the same shoal, but saugers spawn considerably deeper and, usually, several days later.

Fishing Strategies

In waters that hold both walleyes and saugers, you'll need to keep all these biological differences in mind if you're trying to target one fish or the other. There are times when you'll catch a mixed bag, but the fish are normally segregated by depth. Here's how important the depth issue can be:

Late one fall, after a friend and I had a fantastic day of catching big walleyes on river wingdams, the word somehow spread and the report got printed in the newspaper. My name wasn't mentioned, but the next day I got a call from someone who had seen the article. "Did you see the story in the paper about the guys who caught all the big walleyes?" the caller asked. "They must have been saugers—I was fishing there all weekend and we caught a bunch of saugers but not a single walleye."

I then asked him how deep he was fishing. "We caught 'em all vertically jigging in 20 feet of water," he replied. I didn't have the heart to tell him that I was one of the guys who caught the fish or that we caught them by pitching ⅛-ounce, untipped jigs into 1 to 4 feet of water.

Some of the best sauger fishing takes place in early

Although walleyes and saugers may be caught in the same area, saugers usually inhabit deeper water.

spring and late fall, when the fish are concentrated in the vicinity of their spawning areas. The water is cold, below 50 degrees, and the fish are tentative. If you try fishing with a plain minnow, saugers will often grab the tail and hold on. It feels as if you've hooked a weed, but when you pull back, you feel a little life. You can pull the fish in partway, but then it drops off and all you get is a minnow with a skinned-back tail.

I usually fish cold-water saugers with a ¼- to ⅜-ounce jig-and-minnow combination along with a size 12 treble hook as a stinger. Sometimes saugers are just as aggressive as walleyes but, day in and day out, about 80 percent of the fish are taken on the stinger.

Another consideration for springtime walleye/sauger anglers is timing the spawning run. With either species, the prime fishing takes place just before the fish start to spawn. Once spawning begins, the action stops cold. But after the walleye bite has fizzled out, you can still slam saugers for another seven to 10 days.

After a recuperation period of about two weeks, fishing picks up again, but the saugers come around at least a week later than the walleyes.

If you're like a lot of other fishermen, you think of walleyes and saugers as being pretty much the same. But as you can see, that's a big mistake. Until you learn to fine-tune your techniques to match the species, you'll have the same problem as the caller who assumed that nobody else could be catching walleyes because he wasn't.

The Saugeye—A Walleye/Sauger Hybrid

In many waters, walleyes and saugers interbreed to produce a hybrid called the saugeye. It could just as well have been named the wallger, because its characteristics are pretty much halfway between those of the parents.

It not only looks half-walleye, half-sauger, it acts that way as well. The easiest way to identify a saugeye is by examining its dorsal fin. It does not have the black blotch at the base, like that of a walleye, nor the rows of evenly spaced spots, like that of a sauger. Instead, it is mottled. It's usually found a little deeper than walleyes, but not quite as deep as saugers. Its preferences in regard to clarity and bottom type are also intermediate.

The world record saugeye, caught in Fort Peck Reservoir, Montana, on January 11, 1995, weighed 15 pounds, 10 ounces.

The mottled dorsal fin shows that this fish is a saugeye.

THE FOOD FACTOR

If you're like a lot of other walleye anglers, you spend a good deal of time combing the Internet, looking for the hottest new baits, rods and reels or electronics. And, like a lot of other anglers, you've probably been disappointed that this expensive gear didn't produce all the results you had expected.

You can't blame a fisherman for getting excited about the latest toys, but elite anglers pay little attention to such things. Instead, they focus on finding the fish. They know that if they can locate good numbers of walleyes, they can usually catch them.

But finding walleyes is a lot more complicated than ordering tackle. As many frustrated anglers can attest, the fish don't always follow "the rules." There are times when a walleye will endure water well outside its preferred temperature or pH range, and even venture into water with practically no dissolved oxygen, leaving fishermen baffled.

Walleyes violate the rules for one main reason: to find food.

They are opportunists, and their diet may change several times over the course of a year depending on the abundance of a particular food item. Walleyes feeding on shad, for instance, may suddenly switch to mayfly larvae when a big hatch is in progress. And if you continue to use the same tactics you did when they were chasing shad, you'll come home with an empty livewell, regardless of how many new toys you bought.

On the pages that follow, we'll examine how the type of food affects walleye behavior and location.

Yellow Perch

The most important walleye food in the majority of Northern natural lakes, yellow perch couldn't have been designed better for walleye forage.

Like walleyes, yellow perch are bottom-oriented, although young-of-the-year perch often form large schools and feed in midwater or even near the surface.

Perch are also similar to walleyes in that they prefer a firm sand-gravel or rock substrate, but when they're feeding on mayfly larvae or bloodworms (midge larvae), you'll find them scattered over mud flats. Where you find the perch, you'll also find the walleyes.

But there's an odd twist to the perch-walleye relationship. The walleyes are seldom found right with the perch; instead, they tend to school by themselves a short distance away, evidently making short feeding forays to grab a meal and then returning to their resting position.

Yellow perch usually hold tight to a firm gravelly or rocky bottom, but there are times when you'll find them on soft mud or silt.

Yellow perch

When you become familiar with a certain piece of structure, you'll get to know what part of it holds perch and what part walleyes. In many cases, the walleyes patrol the tip of point, and the perch are a short way back from the tip.

Another reason perch make ideal walleye food: Because of the walleye's superior night vision, perch are easy targets under dim-light conditions. This explains why walleyes in clear lakes usually start feeding at dusk and continue well into the night.

Because perch can tolerate low oxygen levels, they're sometime found in very deep water. Walleyes require considerably more oxygen, but they will make short feeding forays into the depths to get a quick meal.

Variability in the size of perch year classes has important implications for anglers. In years when there's a glut of young perch, you'll have to switch to techniques that trigger or tease the fish to bite, such as speed trolling, spinner fishing or rip-jigging (p.91).

Ciscoes

These sleek, silvery baitfish abound in deep, cool Northern lakes. Ciscoes belong to the trout family and, like trout, require cold water. In lakes of moderate depth and fertility, cisco populations tend to be highly cyclical, building up for several years and then crashing during a particularly hot summer. The heat pushes the thermocline deeper than normal, forcing ciscoes into deep water that lacks oxygen—a death trap.

Ciscoes are known for their habit of suspending in open water. Typically, they

Cisco

Dwarf Ciscoes: Perfect Food for Trophy Walleyes?

Walleyes, like any other gamefish, grow to large size on a high-fat diet. And of all the common walleye foods, ciscoes have the highest fat content. So it's not surprising that trophy walleye hunters often focus on cisco lakes.

But if you're willing to do a little homework, you can further increase your chances of finding a big-walleye goldmine.

Ciscoes in certain infertile Northern lakes, for some unknown reason, never reach a size of more than about 8 inches in length. Yet these small baitfish are capable of reproducing just like ciscoes in similar lakes, where they may exceed 20 inches in length.

Not surprisingly, trophy walleyes abound in many of these dwarf-cisco lakes, and there's a good biological explanation. Full-size ciscoes are much too large for even the biggest walleyes to eat. Consequently, some of the lake's productive capacity is, in effect, being wasted.

In the case of dwarf ciscoes, however, even the largest individuals can easily be taken by medium to large walleyes. Because a greater percentage of the lake's food is of a suitable size walleyes grow much larger.

To find a lake with a good population of dwarf ciscoes, contact a field office of your natural-resources agency or ask knowledgeable local anglers.

If you're looking for big walleyes, start by finding lakes with dwarf ciscoes.

suspend in the lower part of the thermocline, or just below it. This zone offers cool, oxygenated water and often holds a concentration of plankton, the cisco's primary food.

When walleyes are chasing suspended ciscoes, forget your normal structure-fishing techniques. The simplest way to catch walleyes suspended in or just beneath the thermocline is to tie on a crankbait that runs at that depth, and start trolling. With a good sonar, you should be able to see a layer of cisco marks, with a few larger walleye marks scattered among or just beneath them. If you see walleyes at 25 feet, for instance, select a crankbait that runs a few feet shallower; walleyes do not

hesitate to come up for a lure but will seldom go down for one.

The size of ciscoes eaten by walleyes varies from lake to lake, but usually ranges from 4 to 7 inches. It's important to use a bait in the same size range as the natural forage, so you may have to do some experimenting. I've found that size and shape is more important than color. I prefer baits with a relatively slim profile rather than the fat-bodied baits used for bass. A deep- or extra-deep-diving crankbait will probably track deep enough with no added weight, assuming you use line no heavier than 10-pound-test mono. You can also reach the desired depth using lead-core line or downriggers.

Although ciscoes generally stay in or just below the thermocline in summer, you'll sometimes see them dimpling the surface to feed on hatching insects on warm summer evenings.

This behavior was the impetus for developing a little-known but highly-effective trophy walleye technique. Of course, there's a story behind it. One of my favorite trophy-walleye waters, a Canadian shield lake in southern Ontario, has yielded dozens of 10-pound-plus walleyes for me and my friends over the years. But our success pales in comparison to a guy we often ran into when we were there. He would bring in half a dozen big fish for every one we caught. We knew he did most of his fishing at night, because he slept all day. But strangely, we never saw him on the lake, despite doing lots of night-fishing our-selves. He was a nice enough guy, but he got a big charge out of frustrating the "pros," as he referred to us.

Luckily, he moved to a different part of the country, so we didn't have to endure the embarrassment any more. We never could figure out what he was doing. But after a few years passed, I got a phone call. It was him; he'd seen an article I'd written in a magazine and decided to give me a call. "Now that I'm not fishing up there any more, I'll come clean," he volunteered. "I caught most of those big fish trolling size 18 floating Rapalas just below the surface—right down the middle of the bay."

His tactic makes perfect sense. Walleyes in that lake feed heavily on 7-inch ciscoes, which surface-feed all over the bay after dark. When we were working shal-low humps and shorelines, he was trolling open water in the middle of the bay, explaining why we never saw him.

Smelt plumes may extend more than 50 feet off the bottom.

Smelt

If you still aren't convinced that food is all-important in planning your walleye-fishing strategy, consider the experience I had a few years ago while trolling for salmon in Lake Superior.

The surface temperature that day was in the mid-50s, ideal for "flat-line" trolling with spoons and minnow plugs. Our lures were run-ning only a few feet deep over 200 feet of water when something grabbed my Rapala. When I reeled the fish in, I couldn't believe

my eyes—it was a 3-pound walleye. While cleaning it, I found its stomach stuffed with smelt. I couldn't think of a more unlikely spot to catch a walleye but, in talk-ing with other Lake Superior trollers, it's not as uncommon as I thought.

This doesn't mean you should go out and start troll-ing for walleyes in the frigid waters of Lake Superior. But it does prove that that wall-eyes will violate all the rules to find a meal.

Although smelt are not a common part of the walleye's diet, they're becoming more important as smelt continue to spread through U.S. and Canadian walleye waters.

Smelt, like salmon, striped bass and many other marine fish, are classified as a *eury-haline* species, meaning they're capable of living in either fresh or saltwater. But how did smelt wind up in so many freshwater lakes? Experts believe that smelt stocked in a Michigan lake in the early 1900s found their way into Lake Michigan and, from there, eventually spread throughout the Great Lakes. They spawned in thousands of tributary streams, draw-ing hordes of fishermen and launching the annual spring dip-netting circus.

Smelt

Because of their long, thin shape, smelt make ideal walleye food.

It doesn't take much imagination to see how smelt became established in so many other lakes. In all likelihood, they were inadvertently stocked by the netters who, after cleaning tubs of the little fish, dumped the entrails, along with fertilized eggs, off their docks.

In North Dakota's Lake Sakakawea, the state Fish and Game Department intentionally introduced smelt in 1971 to provide walleye forage. Soon the big reservoir was teeming with smelt and, by the early 1980s, was routinely kicking out stringers of 8- to 12-pound walleyes.

By the late '80s, however, biologists began to note a scarcity of young walleyes. Department personnel maintained that the decline was more related to water levels than smelt abundance, but smelt deserve some of the blame (p.28). To the Department's credit, they responded with a massive walleye stocking program that has brought the walleye numbers back.

Smelt are coldwater fish. They prefer a water temperature of about 45 degrees, but can tolerate temperatures into the low 60s. They cannot survive in lakes where they have no cold-water access.

Besides the Great Lakes and Missouri River reservoirs, smelt abound in numerous Canadian shield lakes and other deep, mesotrophic lakes throughout the North. They have also been found in the Mississippi and Colorado river drainages and beyond.

Unlike ciscoes, smelt are benthic, rather than pelagic, meaning that they're bottom-oriented and eat foods that live on or in the bottom. But they also have a habit of forming dense plumes that can extend from the bottom nearly to the surface. In South Dakota's Lake Oahe, biologists have netted walleyes in water more than 100 feet deep. Presumably, they were in the deep water to feed on smelt.

It's likely that smelt draw walleyes into deep water in other lakes, too. In Minnesota's Lake Pokegama, for instance, a few tight-lipped anglers troll plugs for big, smelt-eating northern pike at depths of 60 to 70 feet during the summer months. In doing so, they also catch a fair number of walleyes, mainly fish in the 7- to 9-pound class.

Tom Neustrom, one of the Midwest's top walleye anglers, spends a good deal of time fishing Pokegama. He believes the lake holds two distinct types of walleyes: weedline fish and deep-basin fish. The latter, which are the smelt-eaters, are virtually untouched by anglers. Neustrom has noted a definite decline in the number of weedline walleyes since the smelt invasion.

The Smelt Invasion: A Mixed Blessing

The introduction of smelt (a marine species) to inland walleye waters is a classic good news-bad news story. The good news is the sleek, silvery fish provide excellent walleye forage and, wherever they've been introduced, walleye growth rates have skyrocketed. The bad news is smelt are predacious, consuming the eggs and young of many kinds of gamefish, including walleyes.

Just how much impact smelt predation has on gamefish populations is a subject of debate among fisheries biologists, but many feel it can be significant. Soon after smelt became established in an Ontario brook trout lake, for instance, the brook trout disappeared. Subsequent studies revealed that the smelt, which grew to a length of 12 inches in that lake, were eating stocked brook trout fingerlings as fast as fisheries personnel could plant them.

In an effort to curb the spread of smelt, the Ontario Ministry of Natural Resources recently banned the use of live or dead smelt as bait throughout Northwest Ontario. But such regulations can't stop the spread of smelt that are already present.

A look into a smelt's mouth leaves no doubt that the fish are predators.

If you're interested in checking deep-water-walleye potential in a smelt lake, try trolling the lake's deepest basin using downriggers and 5- to 6-inch minnowbaits. Look for smelt plumes with larger "hooks" beneath or alongside them. You may just discover an untapped fishery and, if you do, the walleyes are apt to be big. Small walleyes are much less inclined to use the deep water and to take baitfish as large as adult smelt.

But you don't necessarily have to fish that deep. Most of my experience fishing smelt waters has been in Missouri River reservoirs. In these waters, I catch most of my big walleyes in water less than 10 feet deep. There is a definite deep-water connection, however. The deepest water is in the old river channel, which meanders across the present lakebed. The key to finding walleyes is to locate a rocky, windswept point adjacent to the old river channel (p.110). Walleyes move out of the depths to feed on the points when conditions are right.

This pattern is strongest in late fall, when the water cools into the 50s. Then the smelt move shallow and the walleyes follow, as evidenced by smelt the walleyes cough up when you catch them.

Shad

Shad are the primary forage in many trophy-walleye lakes. Arkansas' Greers Ferry Lake, for instance, has produced many 20-pound-plus walleyes in recent years, including the present IGFA world record—a 22-pound, 11-ouncer. I'm not aware of any 20-pound-plus walleyes that have been grown on a non-shad diet.

Like ciscoes, shad are pelagic, roaming open water in search of plankton. But shad require much warmer water than ciscoes. They abound in big rivers and reservoirs as far north as the southern Great Lakes region. In the northern reaches of their range, however, frigid winter water temperatures cause heavy annual die-offs.

But these die-offs are a blessing in disguise for walleyes. In Southern shad lakes, a high percentage of total shad biomass consists of older individuals, which are too large for walleyes to eat. In the North, practically all

of the shad are young-of-the-year, the ideal size for walleye food.

Lake Pepin, that wide spot of the Mississippi River, is a prime example of a Northern walleye/shad lake. It is a good trophy-walleye producer (by Northern standards), yielding dozens of 10- to 13-pound wall-hangers each year.

Because it is on the extreme northern edge of the shad's range, major shad kills occur each winter, and anglers commonly see masses of the small fish frozen into the ice. But a few survive the winter by concentrating in warmer water around spring holes and power plant discharges, guaranteeing a good supply of brood stock for the coming year.

Shad schools in Lake Pepin are huge, sometimes rippling several acres of the surface, and highly mobile. You never know where a school will show up but, being plankton eaters, they're usually drawn to the windward shore where the plankton collects.

During my days as a fisheries biologist on the Mississippi, I knew walleyes followed the shad, because I always found walleyes along the windblown riprap during electrofishing surveys. Sometimes I'd go home after a day of shocking, grab a fishing rod and head to a spot where I'd seen lots of walleyes. But the results were usually disappointing.

Eventually I discovered that the fish bit much better in early morning. Working shorelines with jigs often produced a quick limit before breakfast. With such an

Gizzard shad

abundance of shad, it evidently doesn't take the walleyes long to eat their fill, explaining why it pays to get out by sunup and fish hard early.

But with shad being so mobile, there's no guarantee that a spot where you catch fish today will produce tomorrow. That's why walleye anglers in shad lakes rely so heavily on trolling. In Lake Pepin, for example, I'd guess that more walleyes have been caught by lead-line trolling with crankbaits than by any other technique.

Southern walleye/shad lakes, while noted for their giant walleyes, are probably the toughest type of walleye water to fish. Although many of these lakes have excellent walleye populations, only minuscule numbers are caught each year, mostly incidental catches by bass and striper fishermen. Very few anglers have been able to come up with a pattern that will take walleyes consistently. Again, the main problem is mobility of the shad schools.

Striped bass, which also feed on shad, are known for

Although shad are not as long and thin as most other baitfish eaten by walleyes, they have soft flesh and soft fins, making them easy to swallow and digest.

In the reservoirs of the mid-South and South, shad (and walleyes) are commonly found along gently sloping clay banks.

their habit of showing up at odd times in odd places, and the walleyes are no different. The most consistent pattern, however, is very similar to the pattern I discovered on Lake Pepin.

In Lake Cumberland, for instance, much of the shoreline above the Wolf Creek Dam, including the dam face itself, is protected by riprap. When the wind blows into the riprap, the shad move in to feed on plankton, and the walleyes follow. The fish bite best in morning and evening, but there can also be a good night bite because of the very clear water.

How Important is Matching the Hatch?

Choose a lure about the same size as the walleye's

Just how important is it to use a lure or bait that closely matches the food walleyes are eating? You've probably read or heard experts say that it's crucial to walleye-fishing success. But in my experience, mimicking the natural food is unnecessary and may even be counterproductive. Walleyes often seem to prefer something different. Maybe they're like humans and get tired of the same old foods.

When I first began to get serious about walleye fishing, I read about their perch-eating habits. So when I got the chance to fish a well-known perch/walleye lake, I decided to seine some small perch for bait (it was legal). To my complete astonishment, the perch didn't work nearly as well as spottail shiners which, I'm sure, were a relatively rare morsel in the walleyes' diet.

Many walleye anglers would say their favorite live bait is the ribbon leech, but these leeches seldom live in walleye lakes. Horse leeches, however, abound in many of these waters. But if you've ever tried horse leeches as bait, you know walleyes usually turn up their noses at them. Another good example of an effective bait that's foreign to a walleye's normal diet is the nightcrawler. Sure, a heavy rain may flush a few crawlers into a walleye lake, but most walleyes rarely see them.

Matching the color of the predominant food isn't necessary either. The fluorescent green, chartreuse and orange lures that work so well in murky walleye waters do not mimic anything in nature—they're effective because the colors are highly visible.

Size, however, is very important. Walleyes are opportunists and will eat most anything they can find, as long as it's about the same size as their usual forage and has a lifelike action. As the season progresses, baitfish grow larger and you can improve your walleye-fishing odds by switching to bigger baits. Conversely, when walleyes suddenly switch to a diet of smaller food, such as mayfly larvae, try smaller baits.

Only a small percentage of the shoreline in Lake Cumberland, and in most other Southern reservoirs, is covered with riprap or natural rock. The next most likely spot to find walleyes is along a clay bank with plenty of fallen trees to provide cover. Shade from the trees, combined with discolored water caused by wave action against the clay banks, gives walleyes the perfect low-light feeding zone. Wind blowing into shore is a turn-on for walleyes in most any lake, but it's especially important in shad lakes, because of the shad's plankton-eating habits.

The longer the wind has been blowing in, the better. Walleyes begin to move in during the first few hours of an onshore blow, and continue to move in as long as the blow continues. If the wind has been blowing in for two or three days, get out there. You might just get in on the year's best bite.

Wherever walleyes are found, they're opportunists; they'll eat practically any aquatic food that is available to them, including many that we haven't discussed here. Food-habit studies have shown them to eat amphibians such as frogs and salamanders; a

variety of worms and leeches; many types of larval insects; roughfish like bullheads, carp and suckers; minnows such as shiners, chubs and dace; and even gamefish like sunfish, crappies and bass. But unless these foods comprise a major part of the walleyes' diet, it makes no sense to

formulate a fishing strategy around them.

Instead, learn the walleyes' major foods and understand their feeding habits in the waters you fish. Then you've gone a long way toward deciphering their often-mysterious behavior and improving your fishing success.

Fisheries with strong shad forage bases typically produce large, fast-growing walleyes.

WHERE THE FISH ARE

After about 20 minutes of watching me zigzag along the breakline with my eyes glued to the sonar screen, my neighbor couldn't stand it anymore. "Plan on doin' any fishing today?" he sarcastically inquired. "I've got a dinner date at 7."

"Just keep your pants on," I told him. "We're not stopping 'til I find some fish."

As we rounded the corner of a sharp point, the screen lit up. "There they are," I blurted out. "Looks like three or four of 'em."

I tossed out a jig and minnow while he opted for a leech on a slip-sinker rig. Within

seconds, both of us were hooked up to decent walleyes.

Since that incident, I've heard no more of his sarcastic remarks about wasting time trying to locate fish. In fact, his new motto has become, "Fish where the fish are."

Not only did that incident convince my neighbor of the importance of locating fish, it also convinced him that the location factor is usually more important than what bait you put on your line.

Here are some important pointers that will help you locate walleyes in different types of water and at different times of the year.

Eutrophic Lakes

Walleyes in these fertile natural lakes spend most of their time in shallow water. The high fertility produces large plankton crops, reducing clarity and creating a shallow-water comfort zone while decreasing the amount of dissolved oxygen in the depths. In summer, it's unusual to catch walleyes in water more than 15 feet deep.

Because these lakes have such low water clarity, sunlight does not penetrate far and growth of submergent plants is minimal.

Many of these lakes have a dishpan basin, so walleyes

Key Walleye Locations in Eutrophic Lakes During...

Prespawn
- Along breaklines just outside the actual spawning areas

Spawn
- Gravelly shorelines that have enough exposure to the wind so the eggs do not become silted over

Gradually tapering point.

Gravelly spawning shoreline.

Postspawn
- The same breaklines that held fish during the pre-spawn period and other irregular shoreline breaks
- Weed flats near a drop-off
- Gradually tapering points

Summer and Early Fall
- Postspawn locations
- Humps
- Rock reefs
- Gravel patches on a mud bottom

Late Fall
- Steep drop-offs
- Deep humps
- Extended lips of points
- Sharp inside turns along the breakline

Gravel patch.

Weed flat adjacent to drop-off.

tend to move a lot more than they do in highly structured lakes. They often relate to subtle structure such as a one- or two-foot rise on an otherwise flat bottom, or a gravel patch on a mud flat.

Mesotrophic Lakes

The "meso" lake category contains some of the county's finest walleye waters. These natural lakes have moderate fertility levels and plenty of clean-bottom walleye habitat.

Compared to eutrophic and oligotrophic lakes (opposite), meso lakes are intermediate in depth and clarity. Many have lush weed growth, which provides ideal walleye cover.

Mesotrophic lakes generally have at least a fair amount of structure, so walleyes normally relate to particular spots rather than roaming about the lake.

Because the water is relatively clear, walleyes tend to be deeper than they are in eutrophic lakes. In summer, walleyes can normally be found at depths of 15 to 25 feet; in fall, they may go considerably deeper.

Most meso lakes do not have adequate oxygen levels in the depths during summer, so walleyes are found from the thermocline on up, usually at a depth range of 15 to 25 feet.

Meso lakes turn over a little later than eutrophic lakes in the same vicinity. The turnover scatters walleyes and makes fishing tough. But late-fall fishing can be excellent as walleyes form tight schools on sharp-breaking structure.

Key Walleye Locations in Mesotrophic Lakes During...

Mouth of inlet.

Prespawn
- Mouths of inlet streams
- Breaklines adjacent to spawning shoals

Spawn
- Inlet streams with rocky or gravelly shoals and deep pools for resting areas
- Outlet streams with the same

type of habitat
- Gravelly, windswept shorelines
- Shallow, gravelly reefs

Postspawn
- River spawners remain in deep pools
- The same breaklines used in the prespawn period
- Shallow points, especially those with bulrush beds
- Irregular breaklines
- Deep mud-bottom bays

Summer
- Mid-lake humps
- Weedline edges
- Rocky reefs
- Ends of extended points

End of extended point.

Early Fall
- Most summertime locations still hold some fish
- Large shallow flats

Late Fall
- Steep-sloping points
- Deep reefs
- Steepest areas of breakline

Shallow bulrush point.

Oligotrophic Lakes

Of all natural lakes, these have the deepest, coldest, clearest, most infertile water. Although the walleye productivity in these lakes is low, they are often lightly fished, so anglers record some remarkable catches.

Most oligotrophic lakes have good oxygen levels in the depths during the summer months, so walleyes can go wherever they must to find food. That could mean chasing ciscoes in 50 feet of water or perch in 10 feet. At night, however, walleyes usually feed in the shallows at depths of 10 feet or less.

Oligotrophic lakes usually have a rocky basin with plenty of structure. While the rocky reefs and points hold lots of walleyes, the fish are just as likely to be found on sandy humps and in sandy bays, because that's where most of the submergent weeds grow.

Despite the clear water, submerged weed growth in other parts of oligotrophic lakes is limited. Weeds cannot take root on a rock bottom, and many areas of the basin slope so sharply that there is no "lip" area for weeds to grow.

Because food is relatively scarce on oligotrophic lakes, inlet streams tend to concentrate walleyes. Baitfish are drawn to stream mouths by the current, and the walleyes follow. In many cases, walleyes move right into the rivers and hole up in deep pools.

Once oligotrophic lakes turn over in late fall, walleye fishing gets tough. With so much deep water available to the fish, finding them is a major chore.

Key Walleye Locations in Oligotrophic Lakes During...

Prespawn
- Flats outside stream mouths
- Breaklines adjacent to spawning areas

Spawn
- Below waterfalls on tributary stream
- Rocky shorelines exposed to prevailing winds

Postspawn
- Shallow, isolated bays that warm early
- Some males remain in tributary pools

Island cluster.

Isolated bay.

Summer
- Deep bays, especially those with sandy shorelines
- Flats at entrance to bays
- Rocky reefs

- Around island clusters
- River mouths
- Sandy, weedy humps
- Suspended in thermocline

River mouth.

Early Fall
- Shallow flats
- Shallow points
- Shallow humps

Late Fall
- Deep reefs
- Extended points with a sharp break at the end
- Suspended in deep water

Big Rivers

Big-river walleyes seldom stay in one spot for long. Not only do they undertake lengthy seasonal migrations, they also move about in response to frequent changes in the water level.

When the water rises, walleyes instinctively move shallower because the newly flooded vegetation holds an ample supply of baitfish. When the water drops, walleyes go deeper to prevent becoming trapped in an isolated pool.

Most big rivers are low in clarity, so walleyes are almost always in shallow water. There is no reason for them to go deep, because the water is thoroughly mixed and the temperature is the same from top to bottom.

The key to catching river walleyes is learning to judge current. Walleyes seldom hold in fast current, nor do they like stagnant water. They spend the majority of their time in slow to moderate current.

My way of judging current speed is to toss a ¼-ounce jig downstream and slowly retrieve it upstream. If I can't keep it on the bottom, the current is too fast for walleyes.

Most big rivers have silty bottoms. But if you can find some exposed rock, there's a good chance you've found some walleyes. Be sure to check natural rock shorelines, riprap banks and wingdams.

River walleyes differ from lake dwellers in that their spawning migration begins in fall. In rivers that are dammed, the fish swim upstream and congregate in tailraces, where they spend the winter.

Key Walleye Locations in Big Rivers During...

Prespawn
- Deep eddies along the main channel
- Deep holes in tailraces
- Areas of the main channel with a "duned" bottom, which allows walleyes to get out of the current

Spawn
- Natural rock shorelines brushed by light current
- Riprap shorelines with an extended lip and small rock
- Flooded trees and brush along the main river channel
- Flooded marsh grass (high-water years)

Postspawn
- Some males remain in vicinity of spawning area
- Sandy, current-brushed points downstream of spawning area
- Flats with slow current adjacent to river channel
- Deep cuts connecting the main river channel to backwater lakes and sloughs
- Deep backwater lakes

Wingdam.

Summer and Early Fall
- Rocky points
- Wingdams
- Riprap banks
- Deep cuts connecting the main river channel to deep backwater lakes
- Deep backwater lakes

Late Fall
- The same spots that held walleyes in summer and early fall, but in shallower water
- Eddies and slow-current zones in tailraces

Flooded trees along channel.

Shallow Reservoirs

These man-made lakes, called *flowages* in the North, were created by damming rivers that flowed through flat country. In some cases, the dam deepened a very shallow lake that already existed.

Most of these lakes are highly fertile, so water clarity is low and walleyes spend most of their time in the shallows. Weed growth is minimal, but there may be brushy flats or standing timber.

These waters tend to be silty, so any rocky or gravelly areas, such as the riprap dam facing or a flooded roadbed, are sure to be walleye magnets.

The old river channel is extremely important in lakes of this type, because it offers the only deep-water refuge.

Mid-Depth Reservoirs

Sometimes called *hill-land* or *highland* reservoirs, these lakes were created by damming rivers in hilly or mountainous terrain, primarily in the mid-South and South. Due to the nature of the landscape, the lake basin is irregular, with numerous creek arms.

Most of these lakes have deep, relatively clear water of moderate fertility. They often have large populations of gizzard shad, meaning that the walleyes can be here today, gone tomorrow.

Mid-depth reservoirs are commonly drawn down in fall in preparation for spring floods. If the drawdown is severe, walleyes are forced into the old river channel. Or they may swim upstream into the flowing portion of the river.

Key Walleye Locations in Shallow Reservoirs During...

Prespawn
- Old river channel at the head of the lake
- Deep water adjacent to riprap dam facing or gravel shorelines

Spawn
- Flooded roadbeds
- Riprap dam facing
- Gravel shorelines

Riprap dam facing.

Postspawn
- Mud flats at upper end of reservoir
- Rocky or brushy points projecting into old river channel

Summer and Early Fall
- Edges of old river channel
- Timbered flats along old river channel
- Humps near old river channel
- Rocky or brushy points projecting into old river channel

Timbered flat.

Late Fall
- Old lake basins, especially those that have springs to warm the water
- Deep holes in the old river channel

Key Walleye Locations in Mid-Depth Reservoirs During...

Mouth of creek arm.

Prespawn
- Mouths of creek arms
- Main-river pools below rapids or dams

Spawn
- Streams at the heads of creek arms
- Below rapids or dams in the main river, upstream of the lake
- Riprap shorelines and embankments
- Dam facings

Postspawn
- Some males remain in spawning streams

- Shallow points in creek arms
- Timbered flats along creek channels

Summer and Early Fall
- Rocky main-lake points
- Rocky reefs
- Suspended in the thermocline

Late Fall
- Steep-sloping areas of the old river channel

Rocky point.

- Deep pools upstream of the reservoir
- Mouths of creek arms

THE EQUIPMENT

*V*eteran walleye anglers do everything possible to tilt the odds in their favor. That means owning the right equipment and knowing how to use it.

DECIPHERING SONAR

"Get ready," I alerted my fishing partner, "there are a couple of fish down there." Seconds later, right on cue, he set the hook and his rod doubled over.

"I can't believe it," he laughed over his shoulder as he fought the walleye. "That's at least a dozen you've called today."

I'd pulled off the feat because of two important factors—the quality of my sonar unit and my extensive experience interpreting the data it displayed.

The marks I'd been seeing on the depthfinder that day would not have been obvious with a lesser sonar. And although they were not the distinct arcs or "Vs" that show up so nicely in the owner's manuals, I knew the fuzzy, brightly-colored spots were the backs of bottom-hugging walleyes. Experience and a thorough understanding of how sonar works told me so.

The Color of Success

The reason I'm such a strong proponent of high-definition color sonar units like I'd used that day is simple: Such depthfinders show you far more detail than any low-resolution or monochrome (black-and-white) unit on the market. An angler attempting to fish with such a lesser sonar is like a guy with 20-80 vision trying to make out fine print without his reading glasses.

Side- And Down-Viewing Sonar

One of the latest advancements in sonar technology has been side- and down-viewing. Rather than create a two-dimensional sonar picture, side-viewing units essentially create a photo-like image of everything in the water column, from surface to bottom, more than 200 feet from both sides of the boat. Aside from covering a much wider swath of the bottom and learning more about the structure below than with traditional sonar, side scanning helps map cover such as weeds, as well as give a clear picture of the bottom substrate.

Down-viewing performs in much the same way, but instead of capturing images of the water column off the sides of the boat, it focuses on the area straight below the transom.

Regardless of the specific manufacturer, this technology displays the strongest echoes brightly, while weak signals appear darker. Objects also cast a "shadow," making it easier to determine their size and position in the water column. The resulting display can show detailed images of baitfish, rocks, brush, and even suspended fish. As an added asset, such units let you move a cursor to anything noteworthy you see on the display and mark it on the GPS, despite the fact your boat never even passed over the spot.

The technology is extremely useful when targeting walleyes holding in shallow weeds or flooded brush. By slowly motoring along the edge of the cover and watching your sonar, you can identify points, inside turns, depressions, and both thicker and thinner areas within the vegetation. Then, you can hold your boat within casting range of high-odds spots and pitch jigs to them without ever running the boat close enough to spook fish.

As an added plus, these units are also equipped with traditional, two-dimensional, down-looking sonar, which means you can toggle between both types of views to get an even clearer picture of what lies below.

Side- and down-viewing sonar function like an MRI, creating photo like images of what lies below and to the sides of the boat.

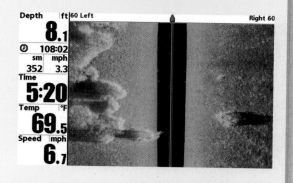

Here's an example of how good the resolution really is. Once, while vertically jigging for lake trout in 80 feet of water and watching the path of my jig on the screen, I noticed a fine line tracking just above the jig. At first, I thought I'd hooked a leaf or some kind of debris, so I reeled in to check the line. It was clean, so I dropped back down again. But the second line was still there. Then I realized that the second line was a tiny size 10 barrel swivel that I'd tied in 2 feet above the jig to prevent line twist.

Resolution is an issue no matter what kind of fish you're after, but it is especially important for walleyes and other fish that spend most of their time on or near the bottom. If the resolution of your sonar unit is not high enough, or if your color palette is limited as in the case of monochrome units, there is no way to definitively distinguish fish from bottom, or tell one bottom type from another.

Here's how to best use your sonar, regardless of its type, to find and catch more fish:

Reading Fish On Bottom

Virtually all sonar units—and the anglers who decipher them—struggle to identify walleyes holding truly belly-to-bottom.

Here's a helpful tip, though: You'll often see what appear to be humps on the bottom

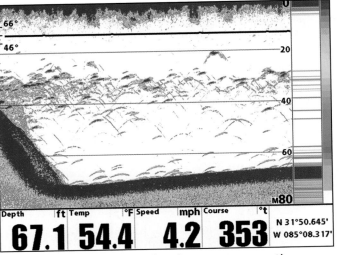

A good sonar unit provides the target separation necessary to distinguish fish holding close to bottom, like those marked here. A lesser depthfinder might display such fish as part of the bottom substrate.

with a little space beneath them. That space means there is water under the object you're graphing, so unless your lake has rocks that float, you're probably marking fish.

However, sometimes this empty space is hard to see—or virtually nonexistent. That's where high-resolution color sonar really shines. That's because such units offer greater target separation between objects, plus the color palette shows more subtle differences in signal strength. In other words, fish will more likely appear as separate from the bottom, while lesser sonar might show both fish and bottom as a singular blob.

But it's important to note that the nature of how sonar works sometimes results in fish appearing to be tight to bottom when they're actually as much as a few feet above it. To understand this phenomenon we need to first review some sonar basics.

To determine depth and suspended objects, the transducer emits pings (sound pulses) toward bottom in

the shape of a cone; the terminal width of the cone is determined by the frequency of the transducer and the depth of the water. The deeper the water and lower the frequency, the larger the cone will be by the time the sound waves hit bottom.

The sonar unit calculates and displays the depth and the position of objects (like fish) in the water column based on the amount of time it takes for the pulse to travel to bottom and bounce back to the transducer. The longer the time elapsed, the deeper the unit perceives the object to be.

The trick is that when scanning relatively deep water, you might mark fish on the outside edge of the sonar cone—fish that are perhaps 20 feet out to the side of the boat. When this happens, the sonar echo takes significantly longer to bounce back to the transducer because the fish is farther out to the side. As a result, the fish is displayed on bottom, when it's really at the same depth as fish you might mark straight below the boat. In other words, the unit is "tricked" into displaying the fish at a deeper position than where it's actually holding. In fact, keep a sharp eye and you'll sometimes spot fish arcs within the bottom reading—or even below it.

To help determine when this is happening, first be aware of the signal strength of the arcs—fish marked well off to the side will usually show up as a weaker

Underwater Cameras

Despite the advancements in sonar, there are some things that simply cannot be totally deciphered by depthfinder alone. Underwater cameras have emerged to fill this void, making them an extremely useful complement to traditional and imaging-style sonar.

The advantages are obvious: Cameras don't leave anything to interpretation as you can actually see what's below your boat, in the same way that you watch television. This allows you to determine the species, size and perhaps even the activity level of fish you're marking on your sonar.

Cameras also show bottom substrate and let you determine the size, species and appearance of baitfish, which helps you better match your presentation to

Underwater cameras help confirm exactly what fish species and cover lie beneath your boat.

the natural forage. Many units can even tell you the depth and temperature at the level of the camera, which is a tremendous help in locating the thermocline.

All of these bits of additional information—which are difficult or impossible to determine with sonar alone—let you complete the puzzle of where fish are holding, what they're feeding on, and how

they're reacting to your presentations.

One of their most valuable—but most often ignored—perks is that they can teach you how to better interpret your sonar because you can constantly compare what your camera shows to what's displayed on your depthfinder. Soon, you'll be able to spot subtle "tells" on your sonar screen that reveal, for example, if the bottom is sand or gravel.

Despite their many advantages, cameras do have a weakness: They require relatively clear water. Extremely turbid, stained or dark waters render them relatively ineffective outside a short range surrounding the camera's lens.

A variety of models are available, from simple, manual models, to motorized versions that deploy and stow at the push of a button.

---

signal. Also, if your sonar unit has the ability, change your transducer frequency; when you're searching for fish, a wide beam, such as an 80 kHz, is the way to go. But when you're picking apart an area, switch to a narrow 200 kHz frequency.

Bugs vs. Fish

While scouting one of my favorite walleye spots last spring, I came upon another boat working the same area. "Anything happening?" I asked.

"Lots of fish down there, but they just don't want to bite," the angler replied, nodding toward his depthfinder.

I was seeing the same marks on my unit, but the

Tips for High-Speed Sounding

Attach your transducer so the face is just below the bottom of the boat and tilted forward at about a 10-degree angle. This way, water will strike the face of the transducer as the boat speeds along.

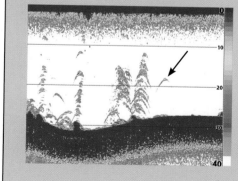

Set your sweep speed, or chart speed, as high as possible. This way, the graph "keeps up" with the speeding boat and a fish makes a relatively wide mark on the screen.

signals seemed a little too weak and fuzzy to be fish. Since there was a pretty good bug hatch going on, I guessed that the marks were actually clumps of insect larvae, so I headed for a different spot.

After catching a nice batch of walleyes, I was on my way back to the landing when I spotted the same guy working the same spot. "Those fish ever turn on?" I asked.

"Nah, never got a bite—can't believe it."

That's an important lesson: Even on the best sonar, clumps of bugs or plankton are very difficult to distinguish from fish. They sometimes make a nice hook just like a walleye, though, causing many anglers to waste their time fishing for phantoms. Keep this in mind to avoid doing the same.

Reading the Bottom

There will be times when you won't be able to mark walleyes because they're truly tight to the bottom or scattered. But you know that they normally favor a hard bottom, so that's where you want to spend most of your time.

You can get a pretty good idea of bottom hardness with any sonar, but a high-definition color unit gives you the most detail. A soft, mucky bottom shows up as a thick red band, often with a feathered top edge.

The band gets thinner and more distinct as the lakebed gets harder. For example, a sandy bottom appears as a moderate red band, while a rock bottom is thinner and more distinct, and you may be able to make out the individual rocks.

An extremely hard bottom often results in a double-echo—a second bottom reading positioned well below the true bottom on the sonar display. This occurs because the substrate is so hard that the initial sonar ping bounces back toward the surface with enough intensity to hit the boat, careen back to the bottom and send another echo to the transducer, creating the illusion of a second bottom.

Recently, while fishing with an old-timer who lives in my neighborhood, he was marveling over all the electronic gadgetry in my boat. As he was dropping his jig to the bottom and talking about how things had changed from the "old days," I saw a mark rising off the bottom to meet the sinking jig. "Hold it right there," I yelled. "He's going to..." Before I could complete the sentence, the walleye rapped his jig and he set the hook. Minutes later he was holding a fat 3-pounder. "That's amazing," he blurted out. "It's just like playing a video game."

How to Interpret Sonar

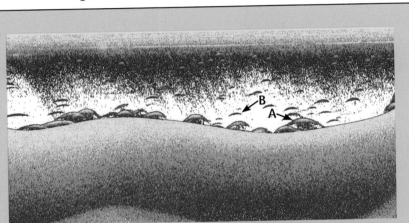

A sharp-edged mark indicates a fish. A large fish (A) makes a thicker mark than a small fish (B).

Bottom-hugging fish show up as a bump on the bottom with a little "air" beneath it (arrow). A rock, on the other hand, usually has no air underneath.

A fuzzy mark usually indicates a clump of insect larvae or plankton rather than a fish.

What to Look for in a Sonar Unit

A depthfinder display should have a minimum of 320 vertical pixels. Some of the best units have more than 600. The more pixels, the better the resolution. More pixels also mean better "target separation." With too few pixels, for example, a pair of small fish swimming close together may appear as one large one. With more pixels, you would clearly see both fish.

A color display. Although black-and-white units certainly work, color displays make it easier to differentiate signal strengths, which means you'll be better equipped to distinguish, vegetation, baitfish, individual walleyes, hard bottom, soft bottom, etc.

The chart speed should be fast enough that fish marks can easily be recognized on the screen at a moderate boat speed (around 7 mph). When doing your shopping, check each unit in "simulator" mode; some will have noticeably faster chart speeds than others.

The unit should have a "gray-scale" or "colorline" feature which makes it easier to distinguish a fish from the bottom.

For detecting bottom-hugging walleyes, choose a high-frequency transducer, which has a narrow cone angle (20 degrees or less). A wider cone (up to 40 degrees) is a better choice for trolling in open water or vertical jigging, because

it allows you to see a large area. Ideally, get a dual-beam transducer, which allows you to toggle between two frequencies to best match how you're fishing.

Other handy features include split-screen zoom, which enables you to view the entire water column on one half of the screen and a blown-up portion of it on the other half.

A wide screen is a better choice than a narrow one, because it gives you more "history." In case you're not paying close attention, you can glance at the screen and see what happened a few moments earlier.

Be sure the unit you select is guaranteed waterproof.

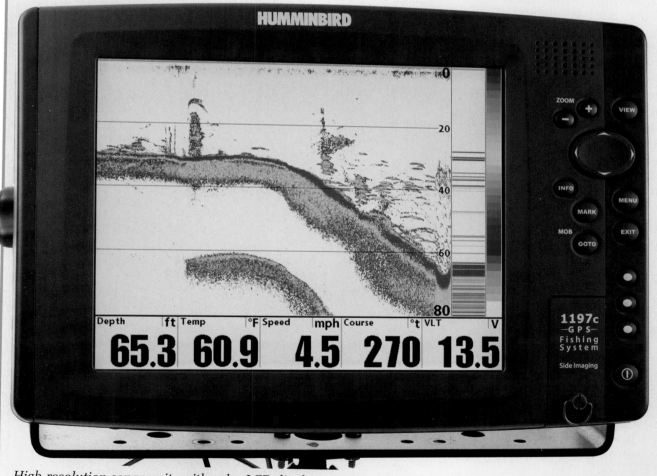

High-resolution sonar units with color LCD displays are the most popular and effective depthfinders. They provide an unparalleled amount of information on bottom content, walleye, baitfish and cover type.

THE ABCs OF GPS

Global Positioning System (GPS) technology has in many ways changed the way people live, work, wage wars—and fish. The system, which operates on signals received from a network of satellites that circle the earth, allows anglers to quickly find productive structure and drop their baits right onto key walleye hangouts.

This is not exactly news. GPS units designed for fishing have been around since the late 1980s. Before that, anglers relied on Loran-C navigators to help them find fishing holes on big water. But despite all the advancements that have occurred since those early days, and the explosion of GPS devices into even day-to-day life, most anglers still don't reap the full benefits of this technology. They either don't understand all of the units' capabilities or they simply haven't been exposed to the methods employed by experienced GPS users.

GPS Lake Maps

When GPS technology first hit the scene, units were basically used to place "invisible marker buoys." The angler would catch fish in a particular spot, or come across a critical piece of structure while using their sonar, and then save the coordinates as a waypoint on the GPS.

Obviously, this was a tremendous advantage because it allowed anglers to return to within a few feet of productive locations again and again. It also let fishermen share information and direct others to key spots. This was helpful on large walleye waters such as Lake Erie, as cooperating anglers could split up until one boat located fish. Those anglers could then contact their partners via phone or radio and give them the coordinates on the spot.

If that spot went cold, the boats could split up once again and repeat the procedure—it was a dynamite method that wasn't possible without a navigation system.

The technology's ability to leave a "breadcrumb trail" in plotter mode also clearly marked trolling paths. If a particular run produced several fish, you could circle back to the start of the same path and follow it exactly—you could even match the precise speed that proved effective on the initial run.

But in those early days, GPS didn't really help anglers find productive spots unless they'd already been there. That's all changed since electronics manufacturers created GPS units able to store and display maps, and since map makers developed highly accurate, extremely detailed electronic maps to accompany these units. These maps can come

Popular Types of GPS Units

Permanent-mount GPS units *operate off your boat's 12-volt power system. They have a much larger screen than a handheld unit, so they are easier to read.*

Handheld GPS units *are popular because of their portability and low cost. But the small screen is a drawback, especially when the unit is in plotter mode.*

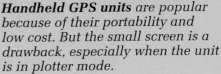

Mapping GPS units *accept cartridges that contain high-definition contour maps of many lakes in a given region.*

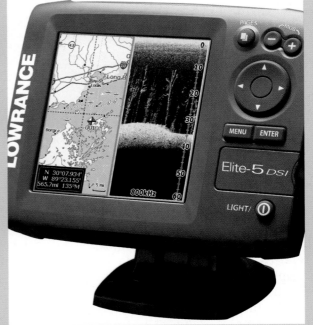

Combination units *can be switched from GPS to sonar simply by pushing a button. Or they can display GPS and sonar signals simultaneously. They save space in your boat by eliminating the need for two separate units.*

pre-loaded on the GPS unit or on aftermarket memory cards that you insert into your GPS.

Now, anglers can not only drop waypoints and plot productive trolling paths, they can see virtually all of a water's structural elements—with contours as subtle as one foot. Rather than search for specific types of structure by driving the boat around the lake, fishermen can now scan the map for likely spots then drive right to them. What's more, when you determine the most productive pattern for the day—for example, walleyes holding on the tips of long, slowly tapering, windblown points—you can scan the electronic map and quickly pinpoint several similar spots.

Plus, when you're fishing the structure, the GPS shows your position superimposed on the map itself, making it easier to determine where most bites are coming, and where fish are most concentrated.

GPS-Based Paper Maps

Even if your particular GPS isn't compatible with high-resolution electronic maps, that's not to say you can't put that same technology to use. That's because many paper maps are now created in the same manner as their electronic counterparts, and they feature grid lines that let you determine the latitude and longitude of any spot on the map.

So, all you have to do is scan the map for a structural element you believe will hold active walleyes, then punch its coordinates into your GPS and navigate to the spot. Once there, use your sonar and GPS plotter to map the larger spot yourself.

How to Navigate Using a GPS Unit

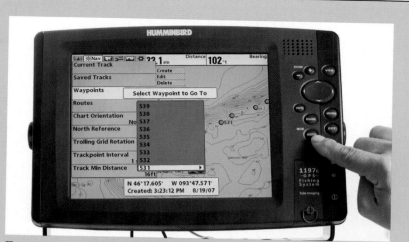

Enter a waypoint by (top) punching in latitude and longitude numbers that you got from a friend, a commercial waypoint log or a GPS map. Or, if you're on the water and find a good fishing spot, simply press the "quick-save" button (bottom) to enter your present position.

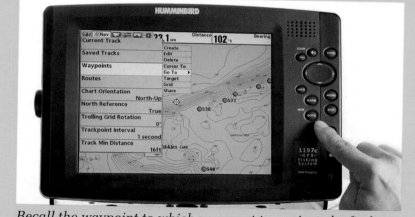

Recall the waypoint to which you want to navigate by finding the name of the waypoint in your log and then pushing "go to waypoint."

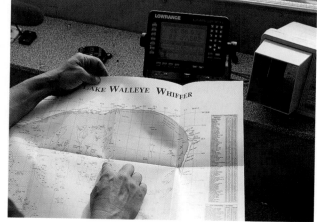

GPS maps have latitude and longitude grids that enable you to determine the "numbers" corresponding to a piece of structure. Then you can punch those numbers into your GPS and navigate to that spot.

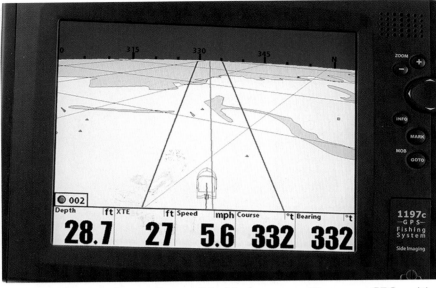

A plotter function lays a fine trail behind your position on a GPS unit's navigation screen as you move. This function lets you plot a safe return route through hazardous areas, repeat productive trolling runs, or backtrack to promising structure you mark on your sonar.

and determine the precise shape of key structures.

Learn to Make a Route

I do a lot of fishing on a large Canadian lake consisting of a maze of islands, bays and channels. Some days, I run more than 30 miles to reach the prime fishing grounds, following deep slots and threading my way through certain narrows to avoid the numerous reefs that would shred my boat's prop.

I know the lake well enough that I can navigate by visual landmarks—under good light conditions. But when it's hazy or I've stayed out a little later than I should, all the islands and cuts start to look alike.

To prevent getting lost and spending the night with the bears—or worse, running my boat up onto a reef— I've punched in a "route" consisting of several key navigational points, including a specific narrows that connects two major sections of the lake, the corner of an island where my deepwater path takes a sharp turn, the mouth of a channel that leads

Here's how:

Set the plotter screen's range to correspond with the size of the structure you're attempting to map. Then, using your depthfinder to stay on a particular contour, follow the perimeter of the structure. Chances are you'll see fingers, bends and inside turns that you didn't know were there.

After you make a few passes over the spot, however, your plotter screen will start to look like a pile of discarded mono. To solve this problem, place waypoints (or icons if your GPS offers them) at every prominent corner along the structure. On my unit, I simply push the "Event Marker" key and then select an icon, such as a flag, to mark those prominent corners. This way I can periodically erase the old boat tracks and the icons remain to show me the shape of the structure.

This lesson applies even if you use a mapping GPS and have high-definition cartography chips for the lakes you fish. Because for as good

as the new maps are, not every body of water on the planet has been mapped, and of those that are, even the very best aren't 100 percent accurate. Some structures are shown as a different shape or size than what's reality, while other productive spots aren't mapped at all.

That's where it's up to every angler to know how to use their sonar and GPS together to map out key areas

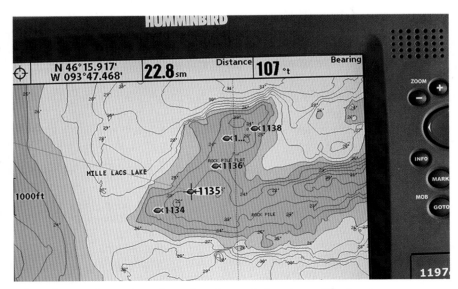

Place icons along the edge of a piece of structure. That way you can clear the plotter without losing the structure's outline.

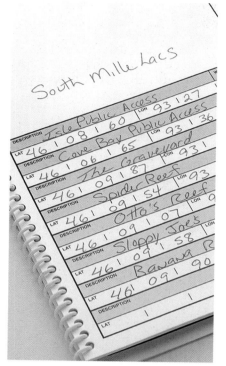

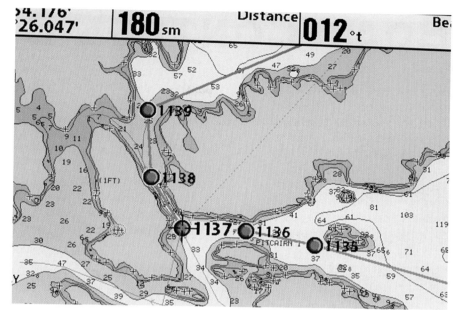

Navigate more safely in treacherous, reef-studded lakes by following a GPS route consisting of several waypoints.

Always keep a log of your important waypoints, along with detailed notes on each spot. This way, should your unit malfunction, your waypoints won't be lost.

back to the lodge, and the lodge itself. When I reach the first point on the route, the unit automatically switches to the second, keeping me off the reefs and leading me home in step-by-step fashion, even on days when I can't see 100 feet. The route can be reversed for running back out the next day.

If you have a sonar/GPS combo unit, you can track the bottom while following your route. I set the bottom alarm to sound at a depth of 10 feet; that way, even if I do veer a little off my course, I won't wipe out my lower unit.

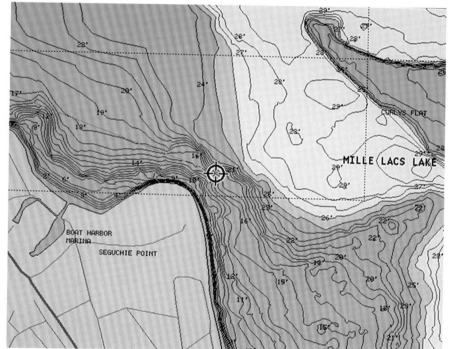

Get the most from GPS technology by equipping your unit with a regional mapping chip. These feature highly accurate hydrographic maps for most bodies of water in a given area, and many of the maps for large or popular lakes show depth changes of as little as one foot.

Make Your Permanent Unit Portable

If you don't want to invest in a handheld GPS, you can mount your regular GPS unit on a "Blue Box" or similar

case designed for carrying an ice-fishing sonar/GPS unit.

I use a hose clamp to secure the GPS module to the handle of the box, and the unit runs off a gel-cell 12-volt battery. Rigged this way, your GPS

can be used for finding ice-fishing holes, or for treks into wilderness waters where you can't take your own boat. And if you have a combination unit, you kill two birds with one stone.

BOAT-CONTROL BASICS

Boat control is not exactly a hot topic on the Internet or in the outdoor press—the phrase just doesn't grab you like "Hottest New Walleye Lures" or "Breakthrough for Trophy 'Eyes." But whether you're pulling a leech along a weedline or jigging a small rock pile, how you control your boat determines if you catch walleyes.

Of all the skills in fishing, boat control ranks near the top of the difficulty scale. Not only is it hard to find good instructional material on boat control, it requires a great deal of on-the-water practice. I've been perfecting my boat-control skills for nearly four decades, and I'm still learning new tricks.

On the following pages, we'll show you the basic principles of boat control, along with some little-known tricks used by the walleye pros.

Why Backtrolling?

You can't talk to an experienced walleye fishermen very long before you hear the term *backtrolling*. There are a number of good reasons for the technique's popularity.

Because outboard motors are geared lower in reverse than in forward, you move more slowly at the same rpms. And your speed is reduced even more because the square transom plows more water than the V-shaped bow.

But the main advantage to backtrolling is that it gives you better boat control, making it easier to follow an irregular contour. The wind does not affect the transom as much as the bow, so you are less likely to be blown off course.

When backtrolling, you'll need a lot of power to push your transom into the wind. Be sure to reverse the head on your trolling motor so it pushes rather than pulls (p.55).

Forward Trolling vs. Backtrolling

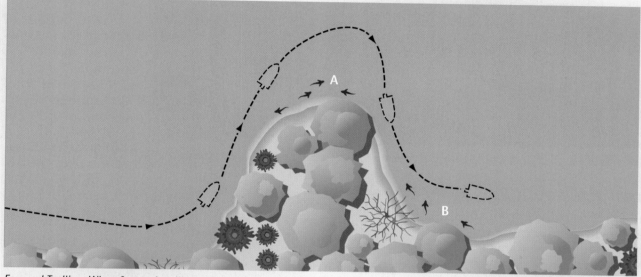

Forward Trolling. When forward trolling along an irregular breakline, you cannot make quick course corrections. By the time you notice a depth change, your bow is past the point where you should have turned, so you tend to miss the critical fish-holding areas. Your line swings wide of the points (A) and cuts off the inside turns (B).

Backtrolling. When backtrolling along an irregular breakline, you can make course corrections instantaneously, so your line passes right through the important fish-holding zones.

Backtrolling with a powerful trolling motor gives you near-perfect boat control.

Trolling-Motor Tips

An electric trolling motor is standard equipment on the boats of most serious walleye anglers. Large, big-water walleye boats, however, are often rigged with a small outboard, because electric motors do not have enough thrust to control the boat in big waves.

Here are some tips for selecting the right trolling motor and using it properly:

Thrust

The biggest question in choosing an electric trolling motor is the amount of thrust. For a boat that weighs 600 pounds (including passengers and gear), I'd recommend a motor with at least 40 pounds of thrust; for a 1,000-pound boat, 60 pounds and for a 1,500-pound boat, 80 pounds. These recommendations may be a little higher than those of the manufacturers, but the extra power often comes in handy.

Until recently, I'd been using a 12-volt transom-mount electric with 42 pounds of thrust for backtrolling. It seemed adequate

Trolling Tips

Reverse the head of a transom mount trolling motor for extra power when backtrolling. With the head reversed, the motor is pushing rather than pulling when you troll in reverse.

When vertically jigging in moving water, use your trolling motor to keep the boat drifting at the same speed as the current. With a downriver wind, you'll have to troll upstream; with an upriver wind, downstream.

for my boat, which weighs close to 1,500 pounds, until I tried a 24-volt model with 70 pounds of thrust. What a difference! Not only does it allow me to fish in a stronger wind, it has greatly improved my boat control. When I do stray off the structure, I can get back on it much more quickly so I don't waste time fishing in unproductive water.

Reverse the Head

When you're backtrolling with a transom-mount motor, even one with ample power, be sure to reverse the head. This way, the motor is pushing rather than pulling. Switching the head around can double your power and increase the motor's efficiency, extending battery life. On most motors, all you need to do is remove a screw, rotate the head 180 degrees and replace the screw. This is an old trick, but one that many anglers fail to do.

Use Two Motors

In a howling wind, even the most powerful trolling motor may not have enough thrust, so you'll have to crank up your outboard. But the problem I've experienced in trying to troll with most outboards is that the steering range is so restricted. Let's say you're trying to backtroll into a quartering wind. Your bow blows to the side and you can't keep the boat on course because the motor won't turn sharply enough to make the correction. You can easily solve the problem by using your trolling motor in conjunction with your tiller-control outboard. Just tighten the tension control on your outboard so you can let go of the handle, and steer with your troll motor.

"Anchor" with a Trolling Motor

If your boat swings uncontrollably from side to side when you're trying to anchor in the wind, the best solution is to throw out two anchors—one off the bow and another off the stern. But what if you only have one? Just use your trolling motor as a second anchor. If you're anchored off the bow, for example, use your transom-mount trolling motor to pull the stern into the wind.

Control Drift Speed

When drifting with the current, use your trolling motor to control your drift speed. In most cases, you want to drift at the same speed as the current. If you're vertically jigging, for example, your line will then stay vertical.

But what if there's a strong downriver wind? Then, you'll drift much faster than the current, causing your line to trail far upstream.

In this situation, turn your transom upstream and backtroll to slow your drift speed until it matches the speed of the current. If you have a bow-mount motor, point the bow upstream and troll forward to compensate for the wind.

Use a transom-mount trolling motor to control your position when anchored from the bow. If the wind is pushing you too far to one side, for example, just turn your motor in the opposite direction and let it run on low speed.

An outboard used in conjunction with an electric trolling motor gives you excellent boat control. The outboard provides the needed power and the electric gives you better steering than you would get with the outboard alone.

Using a Drift Sock

For most kinds of live-bait or jig fishing, a slow, precise presentation is a must. Most anglers know that a drift sock, or sea anchor, will slow their drift speed in a howling wind. But there are many other ways to use a drift sock to improve your boat control.

Slow Your Trolling Speed

When backtrolling on a calm day, you may move too fast on even the lowest trolling motor setting. A drift sock

Drift-Sock Basics

Select a drift sock large enough for your boat. As a rule, a 16-foot boat requires a sock with an opening of at least 42 inches; a 17-foot boat, 48 inches; an 18- to 19-foot boat, 60 inches. A large boat on a windy day may require two drift socks to keep your drift slow enough.

Toss out your drift sock and make sure it opens properly. Attach it to the bow eye or a cleat using a swivel-clip. That way, the sock can spin without tangling your attachment straps.

Pull in the sock by turning it inside out with a second rope attached to the rear of the bag. Otherwise, water resistance makes the sock difficult to pull in.

attached to your bow eye will slow your trolling speed to a crawl.

Keep Bow from Swinging

When backtrolling on a windy day, you're forced to troll into the wind. If you attempt to backtroll with the wind, the bow will blow to the side, making precise control impossible. With a drift sock attached to the bow, however, you'll still be able to stay on course, because the bow won't swing to the side.

Keep Transom from Swinging

When you're attempting to anchor in a river, a strong upriver wind or crosswind may blow your boat far to the side of the spot you want to fish. A drift sock tied to the transom solves the problem, because the force of the current against the drift sock prevents the transom from swinging.

Stay Dry in Big Waves

It's tough to backtroll on very windy days, because the waves splash over the transom. Even if you have splash guards, the spray will soon soak you. Here's a better way: Rig your drift sock with a short rope, no more than 4 feet in length, and attach it to your bow eye. Then troll forward with your outboard; the drift sock will open beneath the boat, nearly stopping its forward progress, and the bow will break the waves so you stay dry. Be sure the drift sock doesn't trail back too far or it will get tangled in your prop.

Drift-Sock Tips

A drift-sock clipped to your bow makes it possible to troll forward into a strong wind and big waves without the bow blowing off course. You can troll very slowly, and the bow will split the waves so you stay dry.

Attach a drift sock to your transom when anchoring in current. This way, the wind (especially an upriver wind) will have less effect and your boat will not swing from side to side as much.

Attach a drift sock to the bow to improve maneuverability when backtrolling in a strong wind. Without a drift sock, your bow would blow to the side when trolling into a crosswind and you would be unable to get the boat back on course.

Clip on two drift socks, one near the bow and the other near the stern, to slow your drift speed in a strong wind.

Anchoring Techniques

The technique of anchoring is definitely not in vogue. In fact, I once heard a tournament walleye angler bragging that he didn't even carry an anchor in his boat.

Make sure your anchor is heavy enough for your boat; otherwise, the wind will pull the anchor through your fishing spot and spook the fish.

Anchoring is not my favorite method either, but it definitely has its place. When you know exactly where the fish are located, anchoring and casting to them maximizes the amount of time your bait is in the strike zone. The other approach would be to repeatedly troll or drift over the spot, but then you risk spooking the fish.

Precision anchoring is an art practiced by only a handful of anglers and information on anchoring techniques is tough to come by. Here are some pointers that I've picked up over the years:

Use a Heavy Anchor

Be sure your anchor is heavy enough and your anchor rope long enough. Otherwise the wind will drag the anchor right through your spot, spooking the

fish. For anchoring on a clean bottom, I recommend a traditional navy-style anchor of at least 20 pounds for a 16-foot boat and 28 pounds for an 18-footer. You can get by with less weight by using a modern fluke-style anchor, such as the Waterspike. A mushroom-style anchor works fine on a muddy or weedy bottom. Your anchor rope should be at least four times as long as the water is deep.

Use Thick Rope

A thick nylon anchor rope is a lot easier on your hands than a thin polypropylene rope, especially when you're lifting a heavy anchor. I normally carry about 120 feet of ⅝-inch soft nylon rope— enough for anchoring in 30 feet of water in a stiff wind.

Attach Your Anchor to a Chain

A 4-foot length of heavy chain attached to your anchor prevents your rope from fraying due to abrasion by rocks. And the extra weight holds the front of the anchor down, so the flukes can dig in.

Anchoring Tips

A lightweight, fluke-style anchor will hold just as well as a heavy navy anchor. The attachment arm is designed to swing up, causing the flukes to dig into the bottom.

Moving your tie-off point will change your boat's position without having to pull up and re-anchor. Moving the tie-off to the right moves the boat to the left and vice versa.

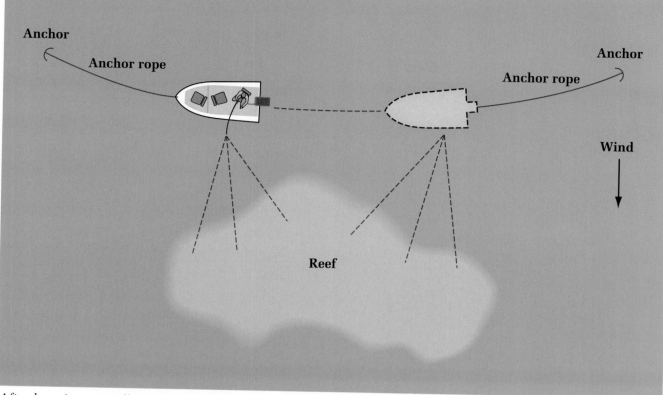

Anchor

Anchor rope

Anchor

Anchor rope

Wind

Reef

After locating a small reef you want to fish, motor upwind of it and drop one anchor off the end of the reef. Then motor to the other end and drop another anchor. Using this technique, you can work your way across the entire reef simply by shortening one rope while lengthening the other.

Tie to the Bow Eye in Rough Water

When anchoring in big waves, always attach the rope to the bow eye. This way, the bow parts the waves so you can ride them out as smoothly as possible. If you tie up to the stern, the waves will crash into the square transom and lap into the boat. I see lots of anglers make the mistake of tying the rope to a bow cleat rather than the bow eye. But with the rope attached higher on the bow, the bow dips lower in the waves. Then a big wave can splash into the boat.

Use Two Anchors to Adjust Your Position

To fish a small reef, motor slightly upwind of it and set one anchor off to one side and a second anchor off to the other side, as shown above. Then you can fish one section of the reef for awhile and move the boat into position to fish another without ever lifting an anchor.

Move Tie-Off Point to Adjust Position

When using a single anchor off the bow, adjust your boat's position simply by tying the rope to a different spot. Tying the rope to a cleat on the starboard side will move the boat several feet to port, and vice versa.

Use Outboard as Rudder

When anchoring in moving water, you can change your lateral position by turning your outboard so the force of the water against the rudder pushes the boat to one side or the other.

Lengthen Rope to Cover More Water

At times, you want your anchored boat to swing widely to cover a larger area. When you're working a large flat, for instance, let out twice as much anchor rope as you normally would. This tactic doubles your lateral coverage.

I've often wondered why you don't hear more pro walleye anglers talking about boat control. I suppose the topic is not exciting enough for a seminar or TV show. Or, could it be they have a secret that they're not too interested in sharing?

Seemingly minor details, such as the thickness of your grub, can make a big difference.

ATTENTION TO DETAIL

Every walleye fisherman knows the feeling: You watch helplessly as the angler in the next boat is hauling in fish one after the other and you can't buy a bite. Your presentation appears to be identical and, try as you may, you can't figure out what he's doing differently. Maybe he's just sitting on top of the fish but, more likely, there is some subtle difference in his technique or the equipment he's using.

Walleye fishing is a detail-oriented pursuit and slight differences may go unnoticed by anglers—but not by walleyes.

Take the time I picked up some new curlytail grubs while on a fishing trip in Arkansas. Leadheads tipped with chartreuse curlytails are dynamite for river walleyes in the North, and I'm always looking for grubs that are a little different. So when I saw that package of chartreuse grubs with silvery, pearlescent reflections, I couldn't resist.

And the Northern walleyes loved them. I don't know if it was the highly visible color or the extremely pliable material, which gave the tail extra wiggle, but they outfished my ordinary chartreuse grubs by a wide margin. One day a friend and I tried an experiment: he fished ordinary curlytails all day and I fished the new ones. We landed 15 walleyes over 7 pounds, and 14 came on the new grubs. The problem is, I somehow lost the package the grubs came in, so I haven't been able to find the manufacturer to order more.

Such minor variations in presentation may not be important in lightly fished waters where the walleyes aren't too sophisticated. But when you're after heavily pressured fish that have seen everything imaginable, details definitely make a big difference.

Here are some tips for selecting walleye-fishing equipment, along with some advice on how to use it to outwit those "educated" walleyes.

What to Look for in a Spinning Reel

A spinning reel with a long, wide spool is a real asset in walleye fishing. It holds considerably more line than a reel with a shorter or narrower spool, so losing a little line to snags is not a problem. You'll still get good casting performance and, when a walleye grabs your bait and starts to run, you can feed line without having to worry about it catching on the lip of the spool.

Another advantage to a wider spool: The line does not form tight coils that impede casting performance.

A front drag is generally smoother than a rear drag, because it has large washers that exert pressure on a flat surface. A rear drag pushes against the drive shaft, which has a much smaller surface area.

Overfilling your reel causes coils to spring off the spool.

A nick in the reel's rim may catch your line and cause a walleye to drop the bait.

Keep The Spool of Your Spinning Reel Full

I know a guy who has been fishing walleyes for years, but rarely has much luck. He invested in a quality sonar/GPS combo and a couple of expensive spinning rods, but his success still didn't improve. When we got together for a fishing trip a while back, I discovered why. "Better spool some more line on that reel," I suggested as we were loading the boat. "Nah, this will work fine," he replied.

We had been backtrolling with slip-sinker rigs for only a few minutes when he felt the first pick-up. As he started to feed line from his half-full spool, I noticed that the line was coming off in jerks, rather that flowing smoothly. He waited a few seconds and then tightened up the line, but the fish was gone. "Darn thing dropped it," he grumbled. "That's the way things have been going."

Had he filled his spool, the fish wouldn't have felt jerky resistance and probably would have held onto the bait.

For live-bait fishing with slip-sinker rigs, I always fill my reel to within ⅛

inch of the rim using limp mono, such as Trilene XL, in 6-pound test. If you fill the spool too full or use line that is too stiff, it will spring off the spool in coils and tangle around the bail or the handle.

Inspect the Rim of Your Spool for Nicks

If you're like me, you toss your spinning outfit into the rod locker on top of half a dozen other rods, or you drop it in the driveway while loading up your truck. Unless you're much more careful with your equipment than I am, the rim of your spinning reel's spool will get nicked, causing the line to catch just as it would if the line level were too low.

Run your finger around the rim once in a while and, if you feel a nick, sand it until it's smooth using fine emery cloth. If the nick is deep, you'll have to buy a replacement spool.

Snub Down Your Drag for Better Hooksets

Most live-bait fishermen use light mono leaders, usually 4- to 6-pound test, so there is

always a concern about break-offs. Many compensate by keeping their spinning reel's drag set loosely, but that's a big mistake. If your drag slips when you set the hook, you may not sink the barb. You get the fish in halfway, and it shakes off the hook.

Here's the solution: Tighten your drag so it doesn't slip at all. Most monofilament line has a stretch factor of at least 20 percent, so you'll seldom break off on the hookset. Be sure your anti-reverse lever is in the off position; this way, you can backreel when the fish wants to take line.

This is the system used by practically all pro walleye anglers. They refuse to rely on a drag for fighting big fish, because even the best drag will stick on occasion. The only problem is that a big walleye can run faster than you can backreel. Be ready to let go of the handle and feather the spool with your finger to prevent overruns.

Use the Right Kind of Live-Bait Hook

For reasons I can't explain, most live-bait fishermen tie their rigs using hooks with

What to Look for in a Jig-Fishing Rod

A 5¼- to 6-foot, medium-heavy power, fast-action spinning rod designed for 6- to 8-pound line is ideal for most walleye jig fishing. This type of rod has better sensitivity than a live-bait rod, so you can feel the subtle "ticks" so common in jig fishing. The short, stiff rod also gives you a faster reaction time; a flick of the wrists sets the hook immediately.

turned-up eyes. Maybe it's because practically every pre-tied live-bait rig you buy has a turned-up eye. Hooks with turned-up eyes are fine, as long as they're snelled on, as they are on most pre-tied rigs. But if you tie them on with an ordinary knot, they're bum hookers.

With the knot positioned at the end of the eye, the point tips back when you set the hook, lowering your hooking percentage. I much prefer a hook with a straight eye, because it pulls the hook directly into the fish. For fishing with leeches and nightcrawlers, I normally use a size 4 or 6; for minnows, I step up to a size 1 or 2.

Straight-eye hook

What to Look for in a Live-Bait Rod

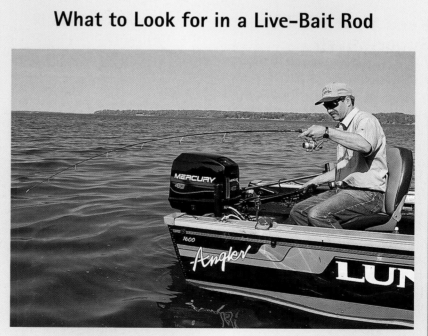

A 6- to 7-foot, medium-power, medium-action spinning rod designed for 6- to 8-pound-test line is a good all-around choice for live-bait fishing for walleyes. With this type of rod, the tip has enough "give" that a walleye will not feel much resistance when it picks up your bait and starts swimming away. Yet you still have enough power to get a firm hookset.

What to Look for in a Trolling Outfit

A 7- to 8-foot, medium-heavy-power, fast-action baitcasting rod designed for 10- to 14-pound-test line is a good all-around choice for walleye trolling.

This type of rod has good sensitivity, so you can feel the action of your lure and tell when it has become fouled. The rod is stiff enough that a walleye usually hooks itself, and long enough that a pair of rods set in holders will cover a swath of water at least 20 feet wide.

Keep Your Hooks Super-Sharp

I almost left this one out, because everyone has heard it many times. But I fish with a lot of different people, and I rarely see anyone using hooks that are sharp enough to suit me. Even some of the chemically-sharpened hooks don't pass my thumbnail test.

If you hold your hook at the angle shown in the photo at right and pull it across your thumbnail, it should catch immediately. If it slides across your nail without catching, get out your hook file or hone. I prefer the triangular sharpening method. Give the hook a few strokes on each side of the point and a few strokes on the back of the point, so it forms a triangle when viewed in cross-section. Keep filing until the hook passes the thumbnail test.

Sharpening a hook this well does wonders for your hooking percentage, but the needle-sharp tip is also

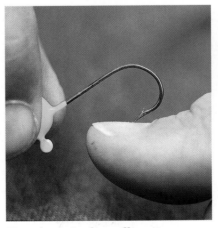

Test the point by pulling it across your thumbnail. If it does not stick immediately, the hook is not sharp.

easier to break off. Inspect the hook often and, if the point is broken, don't attempt to resharpen it because it will be too short and stubby. Instead, touch up and tie on a new hook.

Use Heavier Slip-Sinkers

For some reason, lots of slip-sinker fishermen have the idea that they must use a ⅛- or ¼-ounce weight to achieve a delicate presentation. But try to get down in 20 feet of water in a stiff wind using a sinker that light and you'll be dragging so much line you won't be able to feel a pickup. And even if you do, you probably won't get a good hookset because of excessive line stretch.

With a slip-sinker rig, the weight of the sinker really doesn't matter to the fish. When you feel a pickup, you immediately release the line and the fish swims away. It feels no more resistance with a ½-ounce sinker than it does with a ⅛-ounce. I use a ⁵⁄₁₆ -to ⅜-ounce weight for most of my fishing; but in a strong wind I may go as heavy as

Use a hook file to touch up the two sides and the top of the hook point, forming a triangle.

Use a bigger-than-normal slip-bobber and a heavier-than-normal weight in windy weather.

¾ ounce. This way I can fish with a much shorter line, which gives a better feel and stronger hooksets.

Use Bigger Slip-Bobbers

Most of what you read about bobber fishing these days involves delicate floats that are able to telegraph the lightest bite. But the top slip-bobber anglers evidently haven't been reading those articles.

They use a big slip-bobber that requires a half-ounce sinker to balance it. And if you've ever tried to slip-bobber fish in the wind, you know why.

If you're using a small slip-bobber weighted with a split shot or two, the wind catches your line and prevents the weight from pulling your bait all the way down. The heavy weight, on the other hand, takes it down easily, even in a gale-force wind.

As long as the float has the right amount of weight to properly balance it, a walleye can still pull the float under with no trouble.

Add a Swivel for Vertical Jigging

There's no arguing the fact that vertical jigging is a dynamite walleye technique, but it can also be a real pain. After a couple hours of bouncing a jig up and down, your line becomes so twisted that it coils up whenever you give it slack. You wind up with line twisted around your rod-tip or tangled around your bail, and you have to stop and untangle it every few seconds.

Not only is this tangling an irritation, it can cost you fish. If the line is tangled when you hook a fish, it may break, or you won't be able to start reeling. Luckily, there's an easy solution: Just splice in a small barrel swivel about two feet above the jig. Don't use a heavy ball-bearing swivel; the extra weight makes it difficult to stay in contact with the jig. An ordinary size 10 or 12 swivel works fine.

The average walleye fishermen could spend an entire day in the boat with a professional angler and never notice most of the little things the pro is doing differently. But if you're intent on improving your walleye-fishing skills, you'd better start paying closer attention.

WALLEYE FISHING TECHNIQUES

*V*ersatile wall-
eye anglers
are proficient with
all the newest
methods, but
they haven't
abandoned the
old standbys.

LIVE-BAIT SECRETS

Judging by what you see written about walleye fishing these days, you'd think everyone uses crankbaits, jigs or other kinds of artificials. But the truth is, most walleye anglers still rely on live bait for the majority of their fishing. And when the going gets tough, even the pros break out their bait buckets.

But don't get the idea that live-bait fishing is easy. You've still got to know what you're doing. First of all, you have to make the right bait selection. A bait that works magic in one body of water may not be worth a hoot in the next. And even in the same body of water, a bait that is dynamite in spring may be worthless in late fall.

Another complication in live-bait selection: Most bait shops do not carry a wide assortment of baits; even if they do, there is little consistency in the names of baits, so it's hard to know exactly what you're getting. What one bait shop calls "fatheads," others may call "tuffies" or "mudminnows."

Ribbon leeches may be black, brown or mottled, and all of them catch walleyes.

Walleyes can't resist a wiggling ribbon leech.

Regardless of what live bait you select, it must be fresh and healthy. On the pages that follow, we'll give you some tips for buying or collecting the most popular types of live bait and keeping it in good condition. We'll also show you some bait-fishing tricks that will greatly improve your walleye-catching odds.

Leeches

There are dozens of species of leeches, but only the ribbon leech is widely used by walleye anglers. Surprisingly, ribbon leeches are seldom found in walleye waters.

Ribbon Leech

Most everyone knows that the ribbon leech (*Nephelopsis obscura*) is a first-rate walleye bait. It is the standard variety available at most Midwestern and Northern bait shops.

Ribbon leeches are especially effective at water temperatures above 50 degrees. The reason leeches work better in warmer water is that they're more active then. They wiggle and squirm like crazy, which is exactly what it takes to tempt a stubborn walleye. At colder temperatures, they often roll up into a ball and refuse to swim and, even if they do, they barely move.

Ribbon leeches come in a variety of colors, from light brown to brown-and-black spotted to pure black. The latest leech-selection craze is picking out only the black ones. In fact, some bait shops will do it for you—for an extra five bucks a pound. My advice: Save the five bucks, but make sure you have fresh, lively leeches. Examine them closely, and if they seem lethargic or some of them are covered with white fungus, try another bait shop.

Bigger is not always better in leech fishing.

As much as you hear about jumbo leeches, or "mud flaps," you'd think they're the only ones a walleye will look at. Bait shops love to sell them because they can charge upwards of $3 a dozen. But in most cases, you'll catch as many (or even more) walleyes on large leeches. By large, I mean only about 1½ to 2 inches long when relaxed, and maybe 3 to 4 when stretched out. In contrast—a jumbo leech may stretch out to 6 inches, which means that you'll get more short strikes and miss more fish. In early season, or whenever the fish are fussy, I get more bites on the smaller leeches.

Some experienced walleye anglers take leech selection a step further, as I learned on one fishing trip. A friend and I were slow-trolling an irregular breakline with slip-sinker rigs and leeches. Even though our rigs were identical—same size hook, same size sinker and same length leader—he was catching most of the fish.

It was starting to bother me a little when I noticed him carefully sorting through the leeches. "OK, whattaya lookin' for in there?" I asked. "Tryin' to find a good swimmer," he said, reluctantly divulging his secret. "Some of these leeches swim all over the bucket—ya can't hardly catch 'em. Others just lie there like a blob. I want the lively ones."

How you hook your leech also affects its swimming action. Normally I hook my leeches just ahead of the sucker (the tail end), from the bottom up. This way you're pulling the leech backward and forcing it to swim. But when bait-stealing panfish are a problem, I sometimes hook the leech just behind the narrow head, where the flesh is much tougher. The leech won't swim quite as much, but the pesky panfish will have a harder time ripping it off the hook.

For slip-bobber fishing, I usually hook the leech through the middle, from the bottom up. Hooked this way, it will undulate wildly on the hook, even when the bobber is not moving.

For all of these hooking methods, I prefer a very sharp size 4 or 6 hook with a short, straight shank (p.63). Not only does this type of hook give you a good hookset, it is light enough that it doesn't restrict the leech's action.

How to Hook a Leech

In most situations, hook your leech just ahead of the sucker.

When nibbling panfish are a problem, hook the leech through the tough skin of the neck.

For slip-bobber fishing, hook the leech in the middle.

How to Make and Fish a Slip-Bobber Rig

Slip-bobber fishing is one of the best ways to catch walleyes that are suspended or reluctant to bite. It works best when the fish are schooled tightly on structure, but it can also be used to catch walleyes scattered over a flat.

Most slip-bobber fishing is done with leeches, because they swim enticingly even when the rig is not moving. But you can also bait up with a nightcrawler hooked two or three times through the middle, or a minnow hooked through the back.

Variations on the basic slip-bobber rig include a lighted bobber for night fishing, and a small jig head instead of a plain bait hook.

Most slip-bobber fishermen prefer to anchor their boat just upwind of a school of walleyes they've located with their sonar and then float their slip-bobber rig through the spot. They keep varying their drift until the entire spot has been covered.

A spinning rod from 6½ to 7 feet in length is recommended for slip-bobber fishing. Your line forms a right angle between you and the fish, and it takes a long rod to remove all the slack on the hookset.

Making the Rig

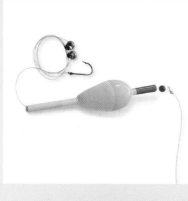

Basic slip-bobber rig. Tie a slip-bobber knot onto your line, thread on a small bead and a slip-bobber, then tie on a size 4 to 6 bait hook or a 1/16- to 1/32-ounce jig head. Pinch on enough split shot to balance the bobber.

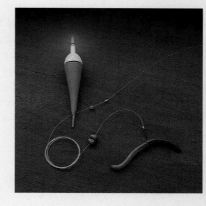

Lighted bobber rig. Tie this rig the same way as a basic slip-bobber rig (left) but substitute a lighted bobber rigged to slip by threading the line through the hole in the bottom.

Fishing the Rig

1 Cast and then feed line as the bobber stop moves toward the bobber.

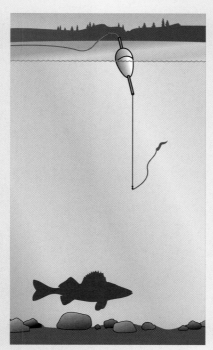

2 Keep feeding line as the bobber stop approaches the bobber.

3 When the bait reaches the desired depth, the bobber stands upright.

A jig tipped with a lively leech is one of the deadliest walleye baits I know, but this combo has not gained widespread popularity. It may be that anglers find it harder to fish than a plain leech on a slip-sinker rig. If you snap the jig too hard, the jig hook often impales the leech and you'll constantly have to reel in and straighten it out. The best way to prevent the problem is to use small leeches, only about 2 inches long, and work the jig with twitches of no more than a few inches. If bait-stealing panfish are a problem, hook the leech through the neck rather than the sucker, just as you would if using a plain hook.

The best way to keep your leeches healthy and thus lively is to keep them cool.

I keep my stash of leeches, usually a couple of pounds, in a 5-gallon pail in a bait refrigerator in my garage. I change the water at least once a week, replacing it with cold well water, not chlorinated city water. You can use city water, but you must first let it stand for a day or two in your refrigerator. Then you'll have the cold, dechlorinated water you need for a water change.

For a day on the water, I carry my leeches in an 8- by 12-inch lunch cooler, the type with the refreezable ice pack in the lid. But even then the water may warm too much on a hot day, so I usually carry some ice cubes in another cooler, adding a few to my leeches as needed.

What happens if you allow your leeches to get too warm?

Temperatures above 55 degrees initiate the spawning process, which accelerates as the water gets warmer. The problem is, once ribbon leeches complete spawning, they die. They won't die immediately, but they soon develop hemorrhages, gradually weaken and then die. If you allow the water to reach about 65, the process is irreversible. In other words, cooling the water will not stop the spawning process. You'll lose your leeches regardless of what you do.

Ironically, the worst leech container you can buy is the flow-through-style bucket specifically designed for leeches. It works fine in spring, when the water is still cool, but it becomes a leech killer in summer.

How to Trap Leeches

1 *Look for leeches in shallow, cattail-rimmed ponds that do not have large gamefish populations.*

2 *Make a leech trap out of a 3-pound coffee can. Put some rocks in the bottom for weight, add fresh fish heads and crimp the top of the can to make a narrow opening.*

3 *Set the can in the water in late afternoon. Leeches will detect the smell of the bait and swim into the can. Pick it up early the next day and remove the leeches.*

Of course, if you're not interested in keeping your leeches after the day's fishing, most any container will do.

Ribbon leeches have a two-year life cycle, spawning in their second year. That explains why the larger leeches are the first to die when the water warms. It also explains why the majority of leeches available in fall are small ones. If you want good-sized leeches in fall, you'll have to get a supply of them in summer and take good care of them.

A jig tipped with a leech is often more effective than a leech by itself.

How to Keep Leeches

1 Store leeches in a 5-gallon pail in an old refrigerator; take out only as many as you need for a day's fishing and put them in a lunch cooler.

2 Every few days, pour the leeches into a strainer and remove any dead ones.

3 Replace the old water with fresh, cold, dechlorinated water. Then add the sorted leeches back in.

4 Do not leave your leeches out in the sun. Even if they survive the heat, it will start the spawning process and they will soon die.

Tiger Leech

Never heard of tiger leeches? Don't feel bad, neither have many other anglers. I made up the term because it seemed to fit these super-active leeches that are easily recognized by the four rows of closely spaced black spots along their back that look like stripes. Normally, tiger leeches (*Erpobdella punctata*) are only about 2 to 3 inches long, even though the books say they can reach 5 inches. But because they're so lively, tiger leeches don't have to be big to be extremely effective. If you try to hold one in the palm of your hand, chances are it will jump out.

You're probably wondering, "Why haven't I seen them and where do I get them?" The answer is, you more than likely have seen them, and you get them at the bait shop, mixed in with the ribbon leeches. The problem is they're very scarce. If you buy a pound of leeches, you may get four or five tiger leeches, or you may get none. The only way I've been able to find numbers of tiger leeches is by walking along riverbanks and turning over flat rocks.

One day, while fishing with NAFC member Dennis Kleve, I found a good-size tiger leech in the leech bucket. "Watch this," I said with a confident smirk, "I've got the secret bait." Seconds after dropping the wildly squirming leech to the bottom, I set the hook on a nice walleye. Kleve shook his head in amazement. "What the heck did you put on there?" he asked. "We haven't had a bite in half an hour."

There have been many incidents much like that since I discovered tiger leeches. I really believe that their intense action makes them more effective than ribbon leeches. Knowing this, maybe somebody can figure out where to get a supply of them. I'd gladly pay twice the price of ribbon leeches.

Nightcrawlers

A 'crawler is a 'crawler, whether it's imported from Canada or picked off your local golf course. I get my 'crawlers from the latter source; not only are they free, but I can select the ones I want. I seem to have a tough time finding decent 'crawlers in bait shops. If you buy them by the dozen, you normally get about six that are big enough to make good walleye bait. The other six are usually about the size of a garden worm, so I throw them away or use them for sunfish bait. When you're paying $2.50 a dozen, that makes each good worm worth at least 42 cents—pretty expensive bait.

The best time to pick your own 'crawlers is in early spring. Wait for a warm, drizzly night, put on your raingear, grab a flashlight and a plastic bucket, and head for the nearest public golf course. But before you go, check to see if they use chemicals to control the 'crawlers (golfers don't like those nightcrawler bumps). If they do, go elsewhere. Private courses are more likely to use chemicals because they have the budget to do so.

Wait until the 'crawlers are completely out of their holes; if they're halfway in, you may injure them when you try to pull them out. In a couple hours of picking, I can usually get several hundred good-sized 'crawlers, enough to last me most of the summer. I keep my 'crawlers in the same bait refrigerator as my leeches. The best 'crawler box I've found is a styrofoam cooler just the right size to fit on a refrigerator shelf. I cut the cooler down to a depth of about 8 inches, fill it with fairly moist worm bedding and cover them with the cooler's original lid. I put maybe 200 'crawlers in that box and the rest in the same type of ice-pack coolers I use for leeches. The big box stays

Tiger leech.

in the fridge and I take the smaller coolers in the boat.

Many walleye anglers don't realize that liveliness is just as important in 'crawler fishing as it is in leech fishing. Trophy walleye specialist Jack Schneider likes his 'crawlers fat and sassy. "If a big walleye inhales a 'crawler, and it doesn't feel the worm squirming in its mouth, it will probably spit it out," Schneider contends. "You may get by with a half-dead worm for smaller walleyes or when the fish are committing suicide, but the big ones are more finicky. Everything's got to be perfect, so if your 'crawler doesn't wiggle around in your hand, or if a perch bites even a quarter inch off the end, put on a fresh one."

Summertime is 'crawler time, but it's also the toughest time to keep your bait in good condition. The worst thing you can do is carry a big box of 'crawlers in your boat on a hot summer day. Unless you keep your 'crawler box in a separate cooler, or use the ice-pack type, your worms will get too warm and lose their zip, or worse yet, turn into a gob of stinky mush.

Earlier, I mentioned the importance of good-sized 'crawlers, but let me explain what I mean by "good-sized." I prefer a 'crawler that stretches out to a length of 7 or 8 inches to a 12-inch "rattlesnake." It's not that the walleyes won't hit the big worms, it's just that you'll miss a lot more of the ones that do. Most walleye experts will tell you that the fish are harder to hook on 'crawlers than on most other live baits, and using giant worms only compounds the problem.

'Crawlers are usually fished on a slip-sinker rig with a size 6 bait hook or on a spinner rig with a 2- or 3-hook harness.

To rig a 'crawler on a plain bait hook, insert the point at the very tip of the 'crawler's nose; thread it down no more than ⅜ of an inch; and then bring it out the side. If the worm isn't centered this way, it may spin when trolled or retrieved. For the ultimate natural presentation, use a 4-pound-test mono leader.

Spinner rigs are often fished on a bottom-bouncer (inset) or 3-way rig.

How to Hook Nightcrawlers—3 Options

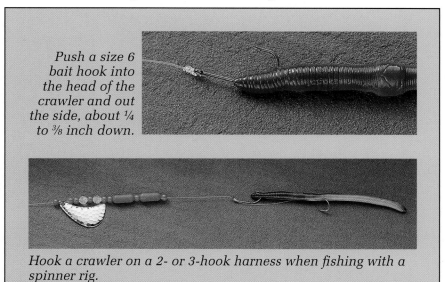

Push a size 6 bait hook into the head of the crawler and out the side, about ¼ to ⅜ inch down.

Hook a crawler on a 2- or 3-hook harness when fishing with a spinner rig.

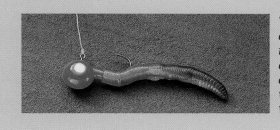

Tip a jig with half a crawler by threading the broken end onto the jig hook, as shown. For large walleyes, use the whole worm.

When slip-sinker fishing, be sure to release line right away when you feel a pick-up. There's no definite rule on how long to wait before setting the hook, but I usually wait a little longer with a 'crawler than I would with a leech. If the fish are really feeding, however, you can set almost immediately; try a couple of quick sets to see. When the fish are finicky, you may have to wait 30 seconds or longer. But if you wait too long, the fish may sense something it doesn't like and spit the bait.

Here's one common mistake I see people making, not only in 'crawler fishing but in all live-bait fishing. Before setting the hook, they slowly reel up the slack and "test" to see if the fish is still there. Then, they continue slowly tightening the line before setting the hook. Chances are, the fish will drop the bait somewhere during that tightening process, and when you set the hook, the fish is already gone. When you think you've waited long enough, instead of testing, start cranking until you feel tension, then immediately set the hook. This way, the fish doesn't have time to spit the bait. Testing accomplishes nothing, other than tipping off the fish to your presence.

There will be times when walleyes prefer a spinner-'crawler rig to a plain 'crawler. As a rule, a spinner improves your odds in discolored water or when the fish are not feeding because of a baitfish glut, a cold front or some other unfavorable conditions.

When using a spinner rig, insert the front hook the same way you would a single bait hook, then push the trailing hooks through the worm so it hangs straight on the harness.

Speed is an important consideration when trolling with a spinner rig. Too slow and the spinner won't turn; too fast and walleyes won't strike. As a rule the best spinner speed is from 0.9 to 1.1 mph.

Slip-bobber fishermen usually rely on leeches for bait, but 'crawlers are sometimes more effective. If leeches aren't working and you think there are some walleyes around, try switching. But don't hook the 'crawler as described earlier. Instead, hook it through the middle so both ends dangle evenly. Walleyes find it hard to resist the writhing worm, and with shorter lengths of the worm dangling, you'll hook more fish.

How to Fish with a Slip-Sinker Rig

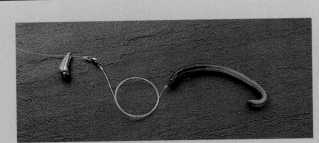

1 Make a slip-sinker rig by threading on an egg, walking or bullet sinker, tying on a barrel swivel and then adding a 3- to 6-foot leader and a size 4 to 6 bait hook.

2 Keep your bail open and hold the line on your finger when trolling. If you feel a tug, release the line and let the fish run.

3 Wait a few seconds, then point your rod at the fish and reel rapidly to take up all the slack. Do not pause and "test" to see if the fish is there.

4 When you feel the weight of the fish, set the hook with a firm wrist snap. If you do not feel weight, just keep reeling because the fish dropped the bait.

Other Popular Live-Bait Rigs

Weight-Forward Spinner. *Usually tipped with a 'crawler, this rig works well for suspended walleyes. Cast it out, count while it sinks and then retrieve slowly. Experiment with different counts until you find the fish.*

Flicker Blade. *Instead of using a pre-tied spinner rig, just thread on a clevis and add a size 0 or 1 Colorado spinner blade (convex side forward). Then thread on some beads and tie on a bait hook.*

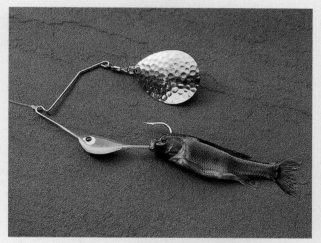

Spin Rig. *Tip this small, unskirted spinnerbait with a leech, half a 'crawler or a minnow. Because of its safety-pin design, it's a good choice for working weedbeds.*

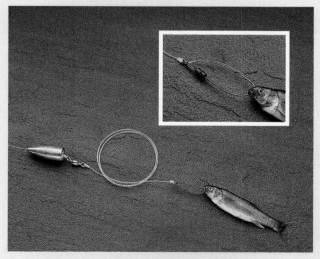

Weedless Rig. *When slip-sinker fishing in light weeds or along a weed edge, substitute a bullet sinker for your egg or walking sinker. In denser weeds, you may want to replace your standard bait hook with a weedless hook (inset).*

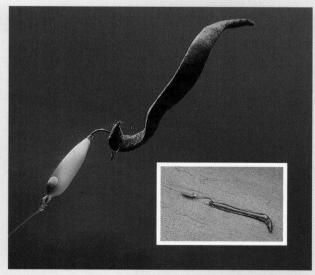

Floater Rig. *To keep your bait above the bottom, rig it on a floating jig head. Or thread a small float onto your line just ahead of the hook (inset).*

Baitfish

Day in and day out, baitfish are by far the most important item in a walleye's diet. And the preference for baitfish grows stronger as walleyes grow larger.

Surprisingly, the baitfish that walleyes feed on naturally seldom make the best bait. Yellow perch, for instance, are one of the most common walleye foods,

but I've never found them to be a particularly effective bait. Maybe walleyes are like humans and prefer some variety in their diet.

Over the years, I've experimented with practically

every kind of baitfish you can name, including not only the usual bait shop varieties, but also a hodgepodge of specimens seined in small streams. Following are my top picks for walleye fishing:

Fathead minnow

Fathead Minnows

These minnows are a staple in most bait shops. They're also called "tuffies" or "mud-minnows." I've even seen them mistakenly labeled as "chubs." Most of the time, any lively fathead makes a good walleye bait. But believe it or not, there are instances where the bait's sex makes a big difference.

A couple years ago, a friend and I were fishing the Wisconsin walleye opener. The water was very cold (in the low 40s) and the "bite" was super-tough. In fact, we hadn't seen anyone catch a walleye, or heard of one being caught.

I was occasionally marking what I thought were wall-eyes on a shallow gravel bar, but nary a tap on a jig tipped with a fathead minnow. Most of the fatheads in our bucket were the black, bumpy headed males, but after dig-ging around awhile, I came up with a plump, silvery female. Almost immediately, a 3-pound walleye inhaled it. After I sorted out three more females and caught three more walleyes, my friend was beside himself. "What are you lookin' for in that bucket?" he demanded. "Females," I replied, feeling sort of guilty. "Whattaya mean females? Lemme see one."

When he put one on his jig, the results were nearly instantaneous. "I've been dragging these males around all morning," he growled. "I drop down a female and it gets hit right now."

Later that evening we brought a limit of eating size walleyes into the fish-clean-ing shack at the resort. We were surprised to see that the cleaning table hadn't been used. Our walleyes were the

Male fatheads (top) are much darker than females (bottom) around spawning time.

only ones caught at the camp that day. If it hadn't been for the female fatheads, the cleaning table would have stayed spotless.

The female fathead phenomenon is most notice-able in spring. I'm not sure why, but I'd guess it has something to do with scent, possibly scent from spawning pheromones. The scent of the female could be more appealing than that of the male, or maybe its just that the silvery females are more visible than the blackish males. Later, when the males lose their spawning bumps and regain their silvery color-ation, I don't see much of a difference.

Fatheads have one big advantage over other kinds of minnows: They're extremely hardy, especially in cold water. At water temperatures of 50 degrees or below, you can keep as many as you want in an ordinary styro-foam minnow bucket with no risk of losing them from lack of oxygen. They simply come to the surface and

gulp in air. They'll also stay alive better than any other minnow in warm water, but you won't be able to keep as many unless you put them in a flow-through bucket or aerate them.

Spottail Shiners

Until recently, I'd never been much of a proponent of any kind of shiner min-now. I just didn't like the idea of paying over four a dozen, and finding most of them dead by the time I got my boat in the water. So I was surprised when walleye pro Tom Neustrom strongly recommended that I bring spottail shiners for an early June trophy-walleye hunt on one of his favorite lakes (sorry—I'm sworn to secrecy). "Make sure they're spottails," he stressed. "Don't get those 'pit' shiners."

Spottails are easy to iden-tify. As their name suggests, they have a prominent black spot at the base of the tail, and bright silvery sides.

Being the stubborn sort, I had to test my usual fare before trying the spottails. But a couple hours of drag-ging leeches and jigs tipped with fatheads proved fruit-less, despite some likely-looking marks on my sonar. Frustrated, I switched to a spottail on a slip-sinker rig.

A spottail shiner has a distinct black spot at the base of the tail.

Spottail shiners are proven big walleye producers.

Within a few minutes I felt a pickup and set the hook. At first nothing moved, but then I felt the big head shakes. Soon, I was admiring a gorgeous 30-inch walleye.

Over the next two days, we boated 13 more walleyes in the 28- to 30-inch class and dozens of smaller ones. Every walleye hit a spottail shiner, despite the fact that we repeatedly tried the other baits. When we ran

out of spottails, we found some "pit" shiners at a local bait shop, but they wouldn't do the job. Spottails were what the fish wanted—period!

Fishing was still good when I came back three weeks later, but spottails were no longer the answer. The fish wanted leeches. You figure it out.

Since that experience, spottails have proven to be a near-magical springtime bait many times, especially in clear lakes when the water temperature is less than 60 degrees. Don't let anybody talk you into other types of shiners, including golden shiners, grass shiners, sand shiners, river shiners or pit shiners. They just don't have the same appeal.

If you're going to use spottails, you must know how to keep them alive. They'll do fine in a flow-through bucket, as long as the surface temperature stays below the 60-degree mark. If it gets warmer than that, keep them in a well-insulated,

aerated bucket and add ice cubes as needed to keep the water below 60. If you add too much ice too fast, however, you'll kill the bait.

Willow Cats

Under the right circumstances, willow cats have astounding walleye catching powers. On the Mississippi River, I've seen them produce stringers of big walleyes in the heat of summer, when veteran anglers using other methods were coming in skunked. Although willow cats are mainly known as a river-fishing bait, I've talked to anglers who have had good success using them in lakes.

What's a willow cat? Its proper name is the madtom, and it's found mainly in weedy backwaters of large, warmwater rivers. One of the smallest members of the catfish family, the willow cat looks pretty much like a small bullhead, but its tail is more rounded and it has a potent venom on its pectoral spines.

For some reason, probably scent, walleyes greatly prefer them over bullheads, although bullheads are a pretty decent bait as well.

If you've ever been "stung" by a bullhead, you know how painful that can be. Well, a madtom's sting is 10 times worse. Once, while pulling into the landing at a popular

Willow cat

Tips for Catching Baitfish

String some pop cans together and sink them below a dock in a river known to hold willow cats. Pick them up the next day and remove your bait.

Catch redtails in a small creek using an ultralight spinning outfit. Rig up with a split shot and a size 12 long-shank hook baited with a piece of worm.

Mississippi River resort, I saw a fishermen lying on the dock moaning.

Some people were kneeling down next to him, and I assumed he'd had a heart attack. Turns out he'd been stung by a willow cat.

If you know how to handle bullheads, you'll have no trouble with willow cats; just grab them with your fingers on either side of the pectoral spine (right).

For bait, I prefer a willow cat about 2½ to 3 inches long. Hook them through both lips using a short-shank, size 4 hook and fish them on a plain slip-sinker rig.

In the 1960s, willow cats were one of the most popular Mississippi river walleye baits and were sold at practically every bait shop along the river. But now only a few bait shops sell them, and they're very expensive. I've paid over 75 cents apiece for them. It's not that nobody wants them; they're just as good a bait now as ever. The problem is, they're hard to

catch and there are no major suppliers.

If you can't find them at a bait shop, you can catch them yourself, using either of two methods. The easiest is to string some pop cans together by tying some strong fishing line to the tabs, and sink them in a shallow, weedy river backwater. Just as big

Hold a willow cat like this to avoid being stung by its pectoral spines.

catfish like to get inside a barrel, willow cats like to get inside something smaller, like a pop can. When you pick up the string of cans the next day, you'll have your willow cats.

You can also catch them with a sturdy dip net. Simply scoop up a netful of weeds from a backwater and sort through it to find the willow cats.

Willow cats may not be quite as hardy as bullheads, but they're among the toughest of all baitfish. They'll stay alive indefinitely if you keep the water clean and fairly cool.

It's a hassle finding willow cats, and even more of a hassle if you get stung. But fishing with them really isn't that dangerous, once you get the hang of it—and the results justify the extra trouble.

Redtail Chubs
Officially known as the hornyhead chub, the redtail gets its name from the reddish margin on its tail.

Redtail chub

With its dark lateral band and dark spot at the base of the tail, a redtail resembles the creek chub but the creek chub does not have the reddish tail. This distinction is important, because creek chubs are a much inferior walleye bait, and I've seen some bait shops label them as redtails.

Among the largest of walleye baits, redtails seem to work best in fall. By then the natural forage has grown much bigger than it was in summer, and walleyes prefer a larger mouthful. I normally use redtails from 4 to 5 inches long. For trophy-class walleyes, I may even go with 6-inchers.

The reason redtails work better than creek chubs, suckers, big shiners or any of the other large walleye baits normally available is their toughness. If you tip a jig with a sucker, for instance, it will be stone-dead after a few casts. But a redtail will stay alive indefinitely. In fact, when it seems to be slowing down, just take it off the hook and put it back into your bucket to rest up. An hour later it will be good as new.

Redtails are found mainly in rivers and are excellent river-fishing baits, but they work equally well in lakes, both natural and man-made. Back in the mid-80s, when North Dakota's Lake Sakakawea (Garrison Reservoir) was routinely kicking out stringers of 8- to 12-pound walleyes, I fished it several times each year. But I always had trouble finding good bait once I got there. Suckers were the only large bait available locally, so I usually wound up using big fatheads.

I finally wised up and decided to bring my own bait. On one trip, I bought 10 dozen redtails and put them in a 10-gallon aerated bucket. Although keeping them cool and changing water was a little extra trouble, the strategy really paid off

Casting ⅛-ounce jigs tipped with redtails onto shallow, rocky points, a friend and I caught 37 walleyes over 7 pounds, including five over 10 pounds and two over 12, on a three-day trip. Local anglers were catching an occasional fish on jigs and fatheads, but the difference was astounding.

The redtail's toughness opens up another fishing option. When slip-sinker fishing, instead of hooking them through the lips or snout as you normally would, try hooking them through the tail. This way, they will struggle to swim against the retrieve, rather than lazily gliding along with it. Walleyes are quick to detect any struggling baitfish, so this hooking method often makes a big difference. If you try hooking most other large baitfish this way, they'll run out of steam within a few minutes and won't swim at all.

When buying baitfish, look them over carefully to make sure they're healthy. If you see a lot of white fungus on their tails, or if they're cruising around near the top of the tank rather than schooling tightly near the bottom, buy your bait elsewhere.

And make sure you know what you're buying. Sometimes the labeling is not specific enough. You'll see a tank marked "shiners," and it will be up to you to figure out which of the 100-plus species of shiners you're getting. Worse yet, the tank doesn't contain what the label says it does. In tanks marked "redtails," for example, I've found stonerollers, blacknosed dace, creek chubs and even suckers. If you blindly accept whatever the proprietor doles out and pay the full price, you're the biggest sucker.

Hook a redtail chub through the tail and pull it backward. The baitfish struggling to swim in the opposite direction often tempts fussy walleyes.

Tips for Using Baitfish

Use an insulated, aerated bucket for shiners and other hard-to-keep baitfish. This model has a battery-powered bubbler in the base.

Catch your own minnows using a wire trap. Bait it with bread and set it out overnight. The minnows swim in through the funnels and can't escape.

Be sure to use a "stinger" hook when fishing a jig and minnow in cold water. The stinger will catch any walleye that strikes short.

Try larger minnows as the season progresses. By fall, many anglers prefer minnows from 4 to 5 inches long.

THE LOWDOWN ON JIGS

I'm a firm believer in the old angling adage, "As a fisherman gets smarter, his tackle box gets smaller."

When I was a walleye-fishing greenhorn, I shelled out a small fortune for one of those giant tackle boxes and filled the 100-plus compartments with every lure that a walleye might conceivably look at. Now, being a jig-fishing fanatic, I can usually carry my tackle supply for the day in a small plastic box that fits in a shirt pocket.

Jigs and walleyes are a natural combination, and for good reason. They are easy to keep on the bottom, and that's where you normally find walleyes.

A jig is the simplest of fishing lures, consisting of nothing more than a chunk of lead or other heavy metal molded onto a hook, sometimes with a hair, feather or plastic tail. But selecting the right jig for your type of fishing may not be as easy as you think. And learning to use a jig correctly is one of the biggest challenges in freshwater angling.

Here's some advice on selecting walleye jigs, along with some tips for developing that jigging touch that many anglers find so elusive.

Selecting Jig Heads

The jig head determines how fast the jig will sink and how well it will hook the fish that strike. It also affects the jig's action. When choosing heads, consider the following:

Head Shape

With these head styles, you'll be able to handle almost any fishing situation:

Round Heads. Standard round jig heads work perfectly for at least 75 percent of the walleye fishing I do. Because of the way the hook eye is positioned in the head, the jig is well balanced, meaning that it hangs horizontally when tied to the line, so it resembles a swimming minnow. Plus, round-head jigs sink quickly, which is preferable most of the time.

Bullet Head. In strong current, a bullet-head jig is hard to beat. Just as a rifle bullet is the most aerodynamic shape, a bullet jig is the most hydrodynamic shape—it slips easily through the current and stays down better than any other type of head.

Slider Head. A slider head jig (one with a horizontally flattened body) is the best choice for swimming over weed tops or any shallow-water obstructions. These jigs sink very slowly and have an attractive gliding action. Some have an upturned nose, for even more lift.

Weedless Head. Fishing in weeds is a problem with most jig heads, because the hook eye protrudes from the top and catches bits of vegetation. A tapered head with the hook eye at the front tip slips through the weeds more easily because it spreads the weeds, running interference for the hook.

Types of Jig Heads

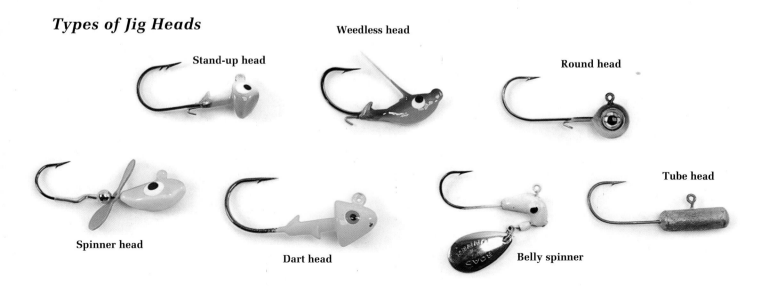

Weedless head

Stand-up head

Round head

Spinner head

Dart head

Belly spinner

Tube head

Stand-up Head. Stand-up jigs are designed to do just that. The bottom of the head is flattened, so when the head rests on the bottom, the hook angles upward, supposedly giving the fish a better look at your offering. In my experience, however, not all stand-up jigs are balanced to actually stand. Before making your purchase, try tossing the jig on a table; if it doesn't stand up, save your money.

Tube Head. These heads are designed to fit inside hollow, soft-plastic tube-baits. You insert the entire head inside the tube and the attachment eye pokes through the plastic. Rigged this way, the tube is firmly secured to the jig head.

Spinner Heads. Some jig heads have a built-in spinner or propeller for extra flash and vibration. The blade also slows the sink rate, giving the fish more time to strike.

Head Weight

The general rule in choosing a jig head is to use just enough weight to reach bottom. If you can easily get to the bottom with a ¼-ounce jig, for instance, try a ⅛-ounce. If you can still get down, but just barely, the ⅛-ounce is the right choice. The lighter head gives the jig a slower sink rate, so the fish get a better look at it.

A selection of jig heads from ¹⁄₁₆ to ⅜ ounce will suffice for practically any conditions you may encounter in walleye fishing. Jig heads are commonly available in ¹⁄₁₆-, ⅛-, ¼- and ⅜-ounce models. But for some reason, most manufacturers do not offer ³⁄₁₆- or ⁵⁄₁₆-ounce sizes. I strongly recommend carrying these in-between sizes, even if you have to mold them

yourself, because they enable you to fine-tune your jigging presentation. Here's how:

Let's say you couldn't quite reach bottom when you switched from the ¼- to the ⅛-ounce head. Then you have the option of trying a ³⁄₁₆-ounce. If you can't find jigs in these in-between sizes, mold your own using products from companies such as Do-It Molds, www.do-it-molds.com.

One big problem in selecting jig heads is that there is little consistency in head weights from manufacturer to manufacturer. A jig that one company calls a ⅛-ounce weighs the same as what another company calls a ¼-ounce. By precisely weighing jig heads, you may find a company that makes those in-between sizes, even

A short-shank jig (top) keeps the bait closer to the jig head than a long-shank jig (bottom).

though they're labeled as something else. If you're a serious jig fisherman, you may want to invest in a precision scale.

Shank Length

The best hook-shank length depends on whether you're tipping your jig with live bait. A short-shank jig is the best choice for tipping; with the jig head closer to the bait, you get fewer short strikes.

The Northland Fireball Jig (p.101) has one of the shortest hook shanks—explaining

---

Recommended Jig Weight*

Water Depth (feet)	Jig Weight (ounces)
5	¹⁄₁₆
10	⅛
15	³⁄₁₆
20	¼
25	⁵⁄₁₆
30	⅜
35	⁷⁄₁₆
40	½

*Note—These weights assume you're fishing under ideal conditions. More weight is needed in wind or current.

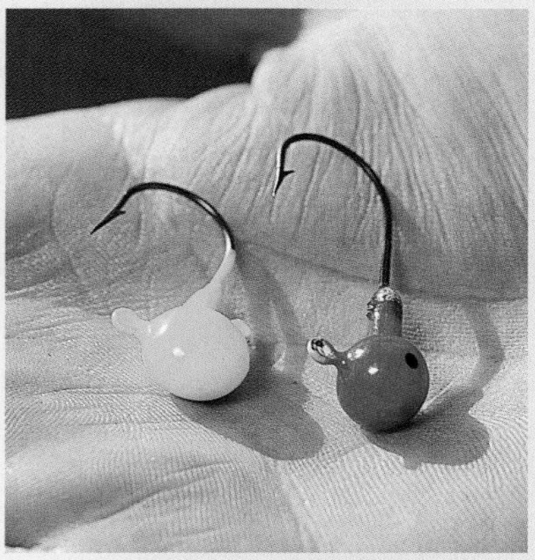

Check your jigs to make sure they weigh what they are supposed to. Both of these jigs are labeled as ¼-ounce, but the one on the left weighs closer to ⅜-ounce.

why it works so well for live-bait fishing. A long-shank hook is a better choice for any kind of jig with a tail. The farther the hook extends back in the tail, the greater your hooking percentage.

Shank Diameter

I prefer a thin-wire hook for most kinds of walleye fishing. Thin wire is best when tipping with live bait because it does less damage to the bait than would a thick hook. And should you get snagged on a log, a strong, steady pull on the line will usually straighten the hook enough to free the jig. The obvious drawback to a thin-wire hook is that you risk losing a big fish, but that risk is extremely minimal. I've seen it happen only a couple times in all my years of fishing.

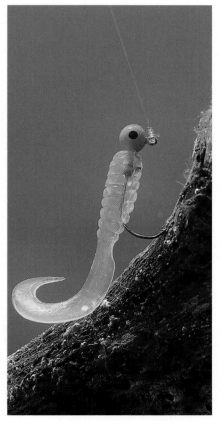

A strong pull will bend a thin-wire shank enough to free the hook.

Hook Size

Many jig heads come with surprisingly small hooks. The idea, I guess, is that smaller hooks tend to be less noticeable to the fish. But if you're tipping your jig with a minnow or a soft-plastic grub, you need a hook with enough gap to make the hook stick well out of the bait. If the gap is too narrow, the point will rest too close to the bait and won't penetrate the fish's mouth.

With a 1/16-ounce jig, I prefer a hook of at least size 4; a 1/8-ounce, size 1; a 1/4-ounce, size 2/0; and a 3/8-ounce, size 3/0.

Selecting Jig Tails

The tail gives the jig its action, adds color and helps control the sink rate. A bulky plastic tail, for example, is much more buoyant than a sparse hair or feather tail, making a jig of the same weight sink more slowly. Here's what you need to think about when choosing jig tails:

Material

Soft plastics have pretty well taken over the jig-tail market. They have great action, look and feel like real food, and are inexpensive. But some softbait tails work a lot better than others. The best ones are very soft and pliable, so the tail wiggles enticingly even on a very slow retrieve or when held motionless in slow current. Softbait tails

A wider hook gap (top) increases your hooking percentage.

come in just about every imaginable style, but you don't need all of them. Here are my favorites:

Curlytails. Also called twister tails or just "grubs," these softbaits have a semi-circular tail with an irresistible wiggle. For the best action, use tails that are very thin. I've had some with tails so thick that they barely wiggled at all. Curlytails are an excellent choice in moving water; the current makes the tail wiggle even when you aren't retrieving the bait.

Shadtails. The body is shaped like that of a shad, and the flared tail catches water as you retrieve, making it wobble enticingly. Shadtails are particularly effective in waters where gizzard or threadfin shad are the predominant baitfish, but I've had good success with them in other waters, too.

Tubebaits. The front half of the body is hollow (a few are solid) and the rear half is split into fine tentacles that give the bait a tempting, lifelike action. Thread tubebaits onto an ordinary jig head or rig hollow tubes on a specially designed jig head (p.86) that fits inside the tube.

Tubebaits work best with a very slow retrieve. By rapidly shaking the rodtip, you can make the tentacles quiver without even moving the jig. They have little action with a faster retrieve.

Bucktails. Bucktail is one of the oldest jig dressings, but is just as effective today as ever. Because deer hair is hollow, the fibers are highly buoyant, so they tend to flare out and have more of a "breathing" action than do synthetic fibers. Bucktail jigs must be well-tied, with a heavy wrapping of thread coated with a layer of epoxy. If you buy cheap bucktails, individual hairs will start to fall out after a few casts. Then the wraps will loosen and all the hair will fall out.

Feather Tails. These jigs may be hard to find and are often more expensive than other types of jigs, but many walleye anglers swear by them. These are also excellent for a technique called rip-jigging.

Softbait Leeches: Live leeches are one of walleye fishing's most effective baits, and softbait imitations look, smell and act like the real thing when fished on a leech. Longer, slimmer versions generally have a more lifelike appearance in the water.

Straight-Tail Minnows: These artificial softbaits have little action compared to traditional curlytail plastics, but they excel when threaded onto a jig, especially for vertical presentations. Some anglers actually add a second softbait minnow, hooked through the head like a real minnow, to add bulk and alter the sink rate.

Tail Size

As a rule, smaller is better in jig fishing for walleyes. But there are times when that is not the case. If your jig is sinking just a little too fast, for instance, try replacing a 3-inch soft-plastic tail with a 4-inch. The extra buoyancy slows the sink rate and gives the fish a longer look at the jig, which can make the difference between them grabbing it and ignoring it.

If you're tipping your jig with live bait, a tail may not even be necessary; in fact, it may detract from the bait's natural attraction. But if you do use a tail, it should be short and sparse so it doesn't cover up too much of the bait. My favorites for tipping are a feather-tail jig, or a small tube jig. It makes little sense to tip a minnow onto a jig with a thick bucktail dressing; the minnow would barely be noticeable.

Types of Jig Dressings

Marabou and plastic

Shadtail

Marabou

Tubebait

Bucktail

Softbait minnow

Curlytail

Softbait leech

How to Fish Jigs

Versatile jig fishermen rely mainly on three different presentations: pitchin', jig-trolling and vertical jigging.

But before we describe these techniques, here are some basic rules that apply to any kind of jig fishing:

- Walleyes generally grab a jig on the drop; unless your line is taut as the jig is sinking, you won't feel the strike.
- What you typically feel is a light tap created by the fish flaring its gills and sucking in a volume of water, including the jig. Whenever you feel this tap, set the hook immediately; if you hesitate, the fish will often spit the jig out as fast as it was sucked in.

- Sometimes the strike is almost imperceptible. The jig just stops sinking prematurely, or it doesn't want to move when you try twitching it. Whenever you feel anything out of the ordinary, set the hook.
- Use the lightest jig that you can keep on the bottom. A light jig sinks more slowly than a heavy one, giving the fish more time to strike.
- You'll need a little extra weight to reach bottom when fishing in wind or current.
- Vary the action of your jig depending on the season and the mood of the walleyes. As a rule, the warmer the water, the more intense your jigging action should be.

In very cold water, you may not want to jig the bait at all.
- Use a stiff, fast-action rod for all types of jigging. This type of rod is highly sensitive, so you can detect subtle strikes. It is also very responsive, so you can get a fast hookset. A softer rod has more "slop," meaning that there's a longer delay between the time you set and the time that the force actually reaches the fish.

Here then are some pointers on each of the important jig-fishing techniques:

Pitchin'

When walleyes are cruising the shallows, they'll spook if you get too close. The best solution is to keep your boat just within casting range, either by anchoring or hovering with your trolling motor, and pitch your jig to them.

To thoroughly work a small piece of structure—such as a reef or extended lip of a point—anchor just upwind in deep water, cast into the shallows and work the jig down the slope.

Anchoring also works well for fishing eddies, pools and pockets in moving water. Be sure to anchor just upstream of the spot you want to fish, then cast downstream and retrieve against the current. This way, your jig has maximum action, especially if you're using a curlytail or shadtail. The current also provides lift, so your jig doesn't snag nearly as much.

To work a long breakline, drift with the wind while casting into the shallows and retrieving down the break.

Walleyes almost always take the jig as it is sinking. If you feel a tap or anything unusual as the jig is sinking, set the hook.

Use a trolling motor to keep the boat drifting parallel to the drop-off.

When walleyes are suspended, try the *countdown* method. Cast the jig, count as it sinks and then start your retrieve on different counts until you determine the right depth. Then stick with that count.

When pitchin' in windy weather, be sure to keep your rodtip low. If you hold it too high, the wind will put a bow in your line, ruining your feel.

Popular Baits for Pitchin'

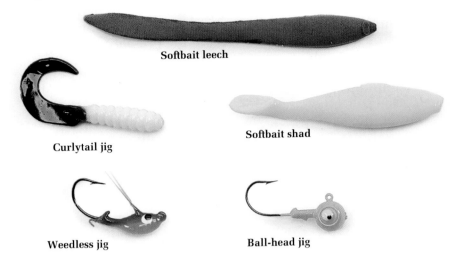

Softbait leech

Softbait shad

Curlytail jig

Weedless jig

Ball-head jig

The Jig Pitchin' Technique

1 Make a long cast and feed line as the jig sinks to the bottom. When it stops sinking, close your bail.

2 Give the jig a short twitch to lift it off the bottom.

3 Keep slight tension on the line as the jig is sinking. When you see the line go slack, give the jig another twitch.

4 Set the hook whenever you feel a tap or anything out of the ordinary. Try to set with a quick flick of the wrists rather than a long upward sweep of the arms.

Jig Trolling

This technique makes it possible to jig-fish a long breakline or large piece of structure without taking your jig out of the water.

The idea is to troll very slowly, working your jig along bottom with a lift-and-drop motion, just as you would do if you were pitchin'. Most anglers who use this method prefer to backtroll to minimize their speed and give them better boat control, but rip-jiggers (below) usually troll forward.

In most jig trolling, it's important to keep your jig in contact with the bottom. If you troll too fast, you'll lose contact. But keep the weight of your jig to a minimum so it sinks slowly on the drop. For the best boat control and slowest speed, always troll against the wind.

When rip-jigging, however, you troll much faster than normal and don't allow the jig to touch bottom. By keeping your jig dancing above the level of the fish, you're more likely to draw a reaction strike.

To troll a light jig close to the bottom, fish it on a three-way rig using a heavier jig, rather than a sinker, for weight. This way you have a chance of catching fish on either jig.

In any type of jig trolling, use only as much line as needed to reach bottom; if you let your jig drag behind the boat, it won't lift off bottom when you twitch it, so it will have very little action.

Popular Jigs for Jig Trolling

Feather jig

Short-shank jig and minnow

Curlytail jig

How to Do It: Rip Jigging

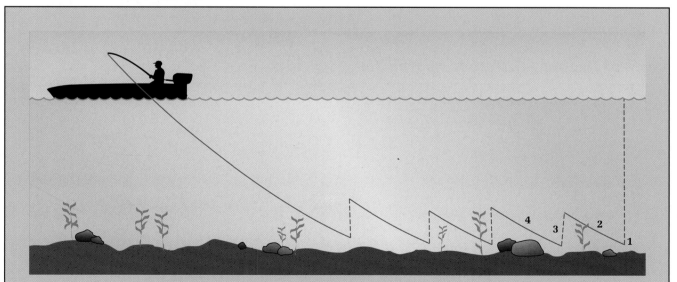

With your boat moving forward at about double the normal jig-trolling speed, toss your jig well behind the boat and (1) let it sink almost, but not quite, to the bottom; (2) give it a sharp snap, pulling it forward 3 to 5 feet; (3) throw slack into the line so the jig sinks quickly and then (4) snap it again. Continue snapping the rod and throwing slack into the line as you move ahead. Set the hook when you feel resistance.

Vertical Jigging

As its name suggests, this technique involves working the jig with your line near vertical as your boat drifts with the wind or current. You can also vertical jig with a bladebait, jigging spoon or tailspin.

The secret to successful vertical jigging is keeping your bait straight beneath the boat. This way you can easily control your jigging stroke and detect even the lightest strike.

How hard you work the bait depends on the mood of the walleyes. When they're active, twitch it a foot or so; when they're not, move it only a few inches or don't move it at all.

A sensitive rod is a must for vertical jigging. I recommend a fairly stiff 6-foot spinning rod with a fast action. Since you're not casting, most any reel with a smooth drag will do, but I like a reel with infinite anti-reverse. This way, when you jig with the anti-reverse on, the handle won't clack on every stroke, as it does on some spinning reels. I use limp 6-pound mono or braid, although many anglers opt for 8-pound.

The most common problem in vertical jigging is short strikes. Most vertical jigging is done when the water is cold, usually below 50 degrees, so the fish are not too aggressive. But you can keep short

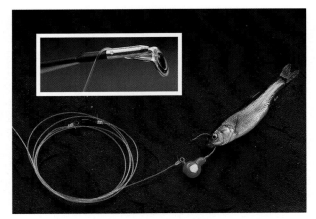

Splice in a size 10 or 12 barrel swivel about 18 inches above the jig. Otherwise, line twist will develop and your line will constantly tangle around the rod tip, as shown in the inset.

Popular Vertical-Jigging Lures

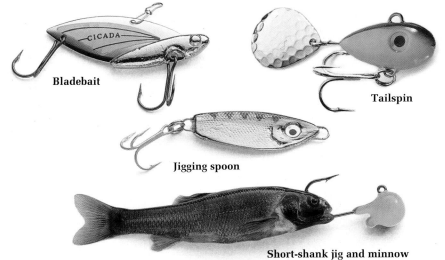

Bladebait

Tailspin

Jigging spoon

Short-shank jig and minnow

Vertical Jigging—Different Approaches

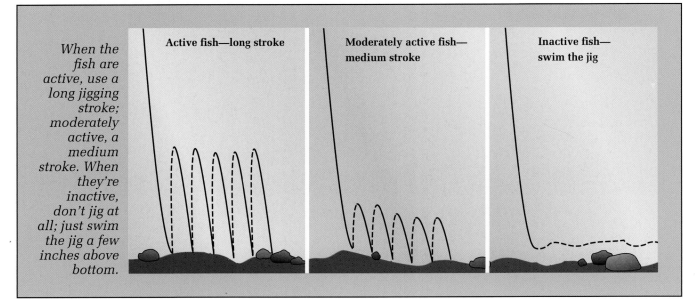

When the fish are active, use a long jigging stroke; moderately active, a medium stroke. When they're inactive, don't jig at all; just swim the jig a few inches above bottom.

Active fish—long stroke

Moderately active fish—medium stroke

Inactive fish—swim the jig

Tips for Selecting Jigs

When tipping with live bait, don't use a jig with a heavy dressing. If you use a jig with a thick bucktail dressing, like this, the bait will barely show up.

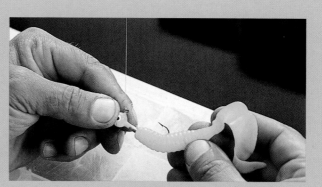

Replace a 3-inch curlytail with a 4-inch to slow the sink rate. Or try substituting a double curlytail for a single.

Choose a jig with a larger-than-normal hook (top) when tipping with live bait. With a small hook (bottom) there is not enough gap between the bait and the hook, so your hooking percentage will suffer.

Select a jig with a tapered head and the attachment eye at the nose when fishing in weedy cover. If the attachment eye is at the top, it will collect bits of vegetation.

strikes to a minimum by using a short-shank jig (p.86) and rigging it properly.

I usually tip the jig with a minnow hooked through the mouth and out the top of the head. The minnow stays on the hook better than if you hooked it through the lips and, with the hook protruding farther back on the body, you'll miss fewer fish.

If, after trying this hooking method, you're still getting too many short strikes, rig up a stinger hook. I use a stinger only as a last resort, because it definitely reduces the number of strikes. Don't poke the treble hook into the minnow's tail, as most anglers do, because it will restrict the action. Instead, just let it dangle alongside the minnow.

Don't push your stinger hook into the minnow's tail. Otherwise, when the minnow flips, the line will cross over its back and pull it into a half curl.

PLUGGIN' AWAY FOR WALLEYES

For a guy who devotes a good share of his life to sleuthing out walleyes on the well-defined structure of natural lakes and rivers, it was a strange fishing trip. I had just spent two days on a Lake Erie charter boat, trolling with downriggers and salmon spoons for walleyes scattered over vast expanses of open water.

Each morning, we'd leave the harbor at Port Clinton, Ohio, and run more than 20 miles to the Bass Islands, where we were catching maybe a dozen decent walleyes a day. Not bad, but not exactly the kind of results I'd been hearing about.

On day three, when we were a couple miles out of the harbor, I was thinking about the long, rough boat ride and the prospect of spending another day staring at the downriggers, so I suggested to the captain that we try something else.

I think he was getting a little bored with downrigger trolling too, so his eyes lit up at the prospect of doing something different. "Want to run some plugs on side planers?" he offered.

I agreed to the plan and suggested that we start trolling right where we were, rather than making the long run to the islands. As the captain steered the boat, I rigged four lines on side planers and ran two more lines straight out the back.

The sonar showed 25 feet of water with some fish scattered from about 10 feet all the way

Plugs excel for covering large expanses of water.

to the bottom, so I chose a selection of crankbaits and minnowbaits that covered that entire depth range.

Within less than a minute, two rods simultaneously sprung to life, and we hauled in a pair of identical 6 pounders. One hit a size 7 Shad Rap running at about 11 feet; the other, a Storm Deep ThunderStick at about 22 feet.

The walleyes were everywhere and at every depth. And it didn't seem to make much difference what plugs we used; they all caught fish.

An open-water situation like this is a plug fisherman's

dream. No other type of lure can cover so much water and such a range of depths.

But there's also another compelling reason to fish with plugs: They catch big walleyes. In one major fishing contest, 42 percent of the trophy walleyes entered over the past 20 years were caught on plugs. Jigs (with or without live bait) accounted for 36 percent and plain live-bait rigs only 8 percent.

On the following pages, we'll show you the most productive plug-fishing techniques for walleyes.

Longline Trolling

When walleyes are scattered along shallow shorelines or over large, shallow reefs, try longline trolling with shallow-running minnowbaits.

Longlining over the weed tops is one of the best ways to draw walleyes out of dense vegetation, and it's among the deadliest of night-fishing methods.

The basic technique is simple; just attach the lure, let out 100 to 150 feet of line and start trolling. To keep the lure out of the boat's wake as much as possible, steer in an S-pattern, pumping your rod periodically to give the plug an erratic action.

When you're trolling in extremely shallow water (five feet or less), the sound of an outboard may spook the fish. But you can get around the problem by trolling with an electric motor. Most shallow-running minnowbaits have their best action at a speed of less than 2 mph, and you can easily go that fast with a powerful electric.

Most shallow runners reach a depth of only two or three feet, but you can go a little deeper by adding one or two split shot about three feet ahead of the lure.

Minnowbaits pull easily and they have the best action on light line, so you can fish them on spinning tackle. A medium-power spinning outfit spooled with 6- to 8-pound mono is ideal.

However, most serious long-liners perfer heavier tackle, such as a 6½- to 9-foot medium-heavy-power baitcasting rod, and a line-counter reel spooled with 10- to 14-pound-test mono or superline.

Popular Longlining Lures

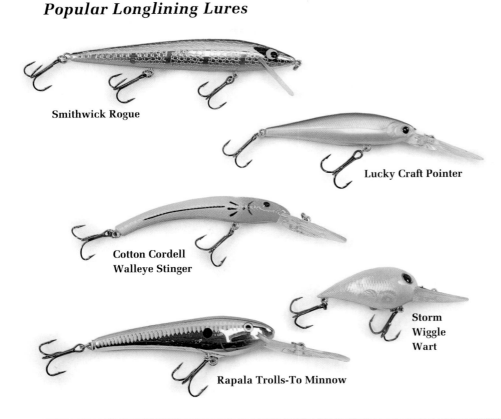

Smithwick Rogue

Lucky Craft Pointer

Cotton Cordell Walleye Stinger

Storm Wiggle Wart

Rapala Trolls-To Minnow

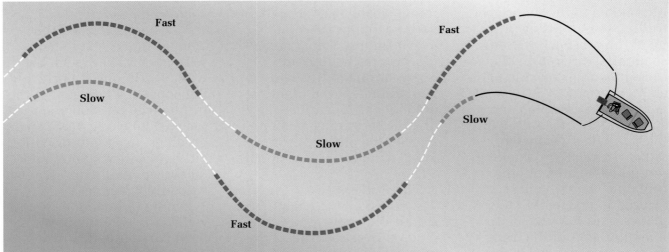

Trolling along an S-shaped course reduces spooking and gives your bait a more erratic action; it slows down on the inside turns (blue) and speeds up on the outside turns (red).

Casting

Casting with plugs works better than trolling when walleyes are concentrated on shallow rocky points, shallow reefs or humps, or around stream mouths. Casting enables you to work the area more thoroughly and reduces the odds that your boat will spook the fish.

Use your electric motor to keep the boat in deep water well off the area you're fishing or, if the fish are tightly concentrated, throw out your anchor. If the fish are holding tight to shore, consider leaving your boat in the garage and donning a pair of waders for the quietest presentation of all.

Casting is usually considered a night-fishing method, but it also works well during the day, especially when it's windy.

Shallow- to medium-running minnowbaits and shad-type crankbaits are the most popular casting plugs. For best results, choose a bait that just ticks the bottom or clears the top of weeds or brush.

It's difficult to cast a minnowbait or even a shadbait into a strong wind, but you can power a vibrating plug (especially the rattling type) into the wind with no trouble. A rattlebait will sink to any depth and stay on the bottom as long as you don't retrieve too fast.

You'll need a medium-power spinning rod about 7 feet in length and 6- to 8-pound to make the long casts that are necessary to minimize spooking.

Casting gives you some retrieve options that you don't have with trolling. You can crawl a minnowbait or crankbait very slowly, pausing periodically to let it float up a little. Or, when the fish are really finicky, you can hang a suspending minnowbait right in their face.

Popular Casting Lures

Rapala Shad Rap

Lucky Craft LVR

Cotton Cordell Wally Diver

Rapala Rattlin' Rap

Plug-Fishing Tips

Attach your plug with a round-nosed snap to maximize its action. A snap also makes it easier to change baits, especially after dark.

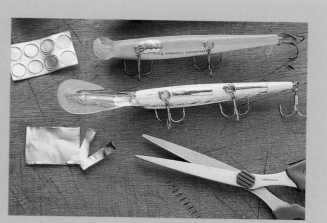

Weight an ordinary minnowbait with adhesive-backed lead dots or strips to make it neutrally buoyant. Golfer's tape will also work.

Trolling with Side Planers

There's no better way to catch suspended walleyes than trolling with side planers. Not only do they make it possible to fish with several plugs and cover a wide swath of water, they minimize spooking by keeping your lines well to the side of the boat's wake.

Gary Parsons, top money winner on the pro-walleye tour and side-planer king, recommends setting up a "trolling grid" that enables you to cover the fish zone horizontally and vertically. Matter of fact, that's exactly what we were doing on Lake Erie that day.

I prefer to rig my planers so they attach firmly to the line and stay attached when a fish strikes. If you rig them to slip down your line, they give the fish extra leverage to throw the hook. And if you rig them to release from your line, you'll spend a lot of time retrieving them.

A 7-foot, medium-heavy-power trolling rod with a light tip and a large-capacity, line-counter reel is ideal for side-planer fishing. The light tip telegraphs the plug's action, so you can easily tell when it becomes fouled.

And the line-counter reel makes it possible to precisely measure the amount of line you're using.

With unweighted lines on side planers, you can reach depths as great as 25 feet and, by adding weight, you can go even deeper. As a rule, a 1-ounce sinker will add from five to 15 feet of depth, depending on the type of plug and your trolling speed.

When you're trolling with several plugs, you can quickly determine the best size, shape, color and running depth. Then you can adjust your spread accordingly.

How to Troll with Side Planers

2 As the boat moves forward, let the board plane out by releasing line from your reel. Lock the reel to stop the board at the desired distance from the side of the boat. Set the rod in a rod holder.

1 Select a plug that runs at the right depth and let out the desired amount of line, usually 125 feet or more. Then attach a side planer intended for that side of the boat and set it in the water.

3 Let out another line and attach a second planer; run it out about halfway to the first planer. Then, set the second rod in a rod holder. Repeat the procedure to set two more lines on the opposite side of the boat (where legal).

4 When a walleye strikes, reel in the line and have your fishing partner remove the planer. Then, you can fight the fish on a free line.

Deep-Trolling Methods

Although some walleye anglers prefer downriggers or lead-core line for deep-water trolling, I normally use a three-way rig.

Unless you're fishing for trophy-class walleyes, downriggers seem like overkill, and operating them effectively really requires a crew of three. Another problem: It's difficult to keep your plug close to the bottom without dragging or snagging up your cannonballs.

There's no arguing the fact that lead-core line is effective, but reeling in a walleye attached to lead-core is a lot like dragging in a stick.

With a three-way rig and a 3- to 4-ounce weight, I can easily get down to depths of 40 feet or more. The rig is easy to fish, I can get my plug down to the fish zone in seconds and I can easily keep it close to the bottom. The heavy weight takes something away from the fight, but a good-sized walleye will still give you a tussle.

For three-way fishing, use a 6½-foot, medium-heavy-power, long-handle trolling rod and a sturdy level-wind reel spooled with 14- to 20-pound-test superline. The long-handle rod helps take the strain off your forearm, and the thin-diameter, no-stretch line makes it easy to get down. It also telegraphs your plug's action much better than mono.

Shallow-running minnowbaits or shadbaits are the best choice for three-way trolling. Deep-diving plugs dig bottom too much, so they pick up bits of weeds and debris.

Although some walleye anglers consider plug fishing a "no-brainer" technique, it has one big advantage over other walleye-fishing methods—it catches more trophy-caliber walleyes than any other technique. So if you're intent on catching one for the wall, just keep pluggin' away.

How to Use a Three-Way Rig for Deep Trolling

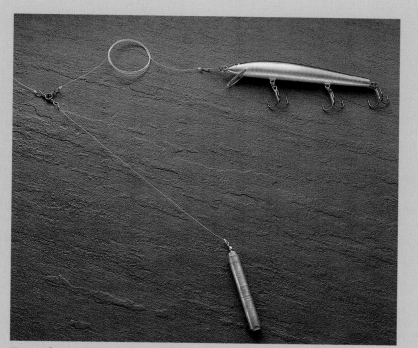

To make a three-way rig, tie on a three-way swivel, then attach a 12- to 18-inch, 12-pound-test dropper with a 3- to 4-ounce pencil or bell sinker to one eye and a 5-foot, 8-pound-test leader with a round-nosed snap to the remaining eye. Clip on your plug.

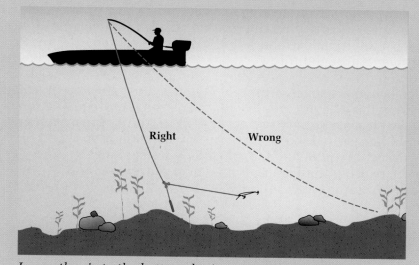

Lower the rig to the bottom, letting out just enough line so the sinker lifts off bottom when you raise your rod. Keep the sinker close to the bottom so it bumps occasionally, but do not let it drag. This way, the plug will run about a foot off bottom.

A River-Fishing Primer

I'll never forget the time I saw a famous TV fishing star trying to catch walleyes in a big river. Every time he thought he had a bite, he threw out a marker. Of course, the current quickly unraveled all the markers, and before long the river was cluttered with floats and strings and other anglers were shouting expletives that can't be repeated here.

The lesson: If you want to catch walleyes in big rivers, forget the techniques you use in lakes and learn the best methods for fishing in moving water.

I've studied big rivers for nearly four decades, through the eyes of both a fisherman and a professional fisheries biologist. I grew up fishing the Minnesota-Wisconsin waters of the Mississippi and supervised fish management activities in those same waters for seven years. Since then I've applied the fishing techniques I learned on the Mississippi to many other big rivers throughout the country.

To become a successful river-walleye angler, you'll need to learn a variety of techniques suited to the time of year and type of habitat you're fishing. Here are the four most important methods:

Vertical Jigging

In most big rivers, walleyes begin their prespawn upriver migration in late fall. Large concentrations of fish spend the winter in tailwaters areas, where they spawn the following spring. The walleyes seldom hold in fast current, opting instead to rest in slower water along the margins of the main channel, usually at depths of 12 to 20 feet.

By far the most productive technique in this situation is vertical jigging (p.92) with a jig and minnow or a blade-bait. Simply twitch the bait vertically so it hops along the bottom while the boat drifts downstream with the current. When the water temperature is below 40 degrees, however, you'll often get more strikes if you swim the jig a few inches off bottom without twitching it at all. A blade-bait is usually worked with longer sweeps than a jig.

Be sure to keep your line close to vertical. If there is no wind and you're drifting in an even current, that shouldn't be a problem. But most of the time, conditions are not ideal; you'll have to contend with wind or conflicting currents that push your boat at a different speed than your line, causing the bait to trail far upstream or downstream. You won't be able to regulate the bait's vertical movement and, if you do get a strike, you probably won't feel it.

The best way to keep your line vertical is to use an electric motor to control the speed of your drift. If the wind is blowing downstream, point the motor upstream and vice versa.

Experiment with different jig and blade colors. My usual choice is chartreuse, but there are times when I've had better luck on lime green, fluorescent orange, white or luminescent (glow-in-the-dark) heads. If the fish are striking short, don't hesitate to add a stinger hook to your jig.

Tips for Vertical Jigging

Position your knot at the top of the hook eye to make the jig swim horizontally. If the knot slips around to the front of the eye, the jig will hang vertically and draw fewer strikes.

Popular baits include (1) jig and minnow with stinger hook, (2) jig and minnow without stinger, (3) dressed jig and minnow hooked through lips and (4) ½-ounce bladebait.

Lead-line Trolling

Lately, I've been reading a lot about lead-line trolling in the serious fishing magazines. Evidently the writers think it's something new. But the truth is, the technique has been around for decades.

It was back in the 1950s when I learned about the technique from Cully Larson, an old "river rat" who ran a boat livery on the Mississippi. I got to know Cully pretty well because I regularly rented one of his boats. To look at Cully's portly frame in a huge pair of bib overalls, you'd never guess that he was such an accomplished river fisherman.

Cully spent more time fishing than he did tending the boat livery, and it was a rare day when he didn't come back with a limit of hefty walleyes. Even though there were no depthfinders in those days, he knew every inch of the river's bottom. "They're stacked up in the trench out by the second red buoy," he'd say, trying to help anyone who was interested. Of course, his wisdom was of limited value to most of us, because we didn't know the bottom contours like he did.

Lead-line trolling was the only technique I ever knew Cully to use. He'd push his boat off shore, motor out a short distance and then start letting out line. He used a 5-foot solid-fiberglass "broomstick" rod and a big Ocean City level-wind reel filled with 40-pound-test metered lead-core line. He tied a barrel swivel to the end of the lead-core and then attached a 3- to 4-foot leader of 20-pound mono. His favorite lure was a green-and-white Cisco Kid, but he sometimes tried other popular baits of the time, including Lazy Ikes, L & S Mirrolures, Brook's Reefers and Heddon Sonics.

Cully's technique was not much different than that of today's lead-line trollers. The main differences are that the 5-foot broomstick has been replaced by a 6-plus-foot heavy-power graphite rod, and the lure selection is a little different

All you have to do is let out just enough line so you

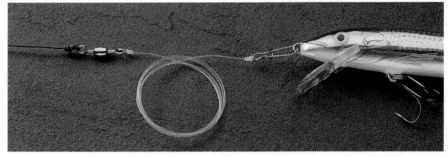

The basic lead-line rig consists of a 4- to 5-foot leader of 20-pound mono attached to the lead-line with a size 4 barrel swivel. Tie a round-nosed snap to the end of your leader to get maximum action from your lure.

Popular Lead-Lining Baits

Lindy Shadling

Cotton Cordell Super Spot

Rapala X-Rap Shad

Original Floating Rapala

Smithwick Rogue

Berkley Flicker Shad

Lead-lining may not be the most sporting method for river walleyes, but it's one of the most effective.

can feel the plug ticking the bottom, then reel up a turn or two. Always troll upstream, against the current, to give the plug maximum action. As you troll, let out or take in line as needed to keep up with depth changes. The metered line changes color every 10 yards, so once you determine the right amount of line for a particular trolling run, remember the color. Then you can let out to that same color the next time you fish that run.

Lead-line trolling works well throughout the open-water season, and it enables

When trolling over a flat, set a pair of lead-lining rods in horizontal rod holders. This way you can cover a much wider swath of water.

you to cover a lot of water in a hurry to locate fish.

If you're not enamored with the idea of trolling with such a heavy rig, try a three-way rig (p.99) with a 3-ounce

pencil-lead sinker or a heavy jig for weight. The thin-diameter line cuts through the current, and the sinker or jig slides easily over a snaggy bottom.

Fishing Wingdams

Big rivers that carry barge traffic often have wingdams—man-made current deflectors that funnel the current toward the center of the river to keep the main channel scoured out. Wingdams are generally made of rocks and usually top out from one to five feet deep; you can easily spot them by the noticeable bulge or rippled area on the surface. A few wingdams top out as deep as eight feet and, in some rivers, they protrude above the surface. Although most anglers assume that walleyes hold in the large eddy that forms downstream of a wingdam, the majority are found in the smaller eddy that forms just upstream of it.

You may have to check 20 wingdams, however, to find one that holds walleyes. The perfect wingdam has moderate current and plenty of clean rock. If the current is too slow, the rocks become covered with sediment and the fish go elsewhere. Nor will walleyes hold on a wingdam where the current is too fast.

Where you fish along the length of a wingdam makes a big difference. As a rule, the current is slowest on the shore end of a wingdam and fastest on the channel end. The idea is to try and find the position where the current is just right. Wingdams may hold walleyes any time of the year, but I've had the

A curlytail jig with a light-wire hook is the ideal wingdam lure. If the hook snags up in the rocks, a strong pull will straighten it enough to free the jig.

most success fishing them in late fall, especially when the water is low. Don't attempt to fish them in high water; then, every wingdam is too fast.

Troll a minnowbait or shadbait on a three-way rig parallel to the upper lip of a wingdam. Keep the bait near the bottom and vary your distance above the wingdam.

Some fishermen prefer to work a wingdam by holding above it with a trolling motor and then casting to it. But anchoring enables you to fish it much more thoroughly. Drop anchor far enough upstream that your boat stops within easy casting distance of the top of the wingdam, and cast to it with a ⅛- to ¼-ounce jig tipped with a curlytail grub.

Your jig selection is critical. The head should have a light-wire hook that will bend a little when you get snagged. The curlytail should be made of very thin, very soft plastic so it will wiggle in a light current even when you're not retrieving it. I normally use a 3-inch tail, but in very slow current I may go with a 4-inch. The bulkier tail has more buoyancy, so it sinks more slowly, giving the fish a better look at it.

Here's my standard advice on color for big-river walleyes: Any color is OK as long as it's chartreuse.

Actually, there's a bit more to it than that. For the jig head, I experiment with plain chartreuse, plain yellow or chartreuse with a splotch of orange or green. My favorite tail color is neon-chartreuse or pearl-chartreuse. This color can be hard to find, but it seems to work better than the ordinary translucent chartreuse tails. When the water is muddy and visibility is only a few inches, I've found white to be the best choice.

Cast the jig downstream over the top of the wingdam and then retrieve it with very short twitches, no more than a few inches long, followed by pauses to let the jig drop back to the bottom. If you can't feel a ¼-ounce jig touch bottom on the pause,

Understanding Wingdams

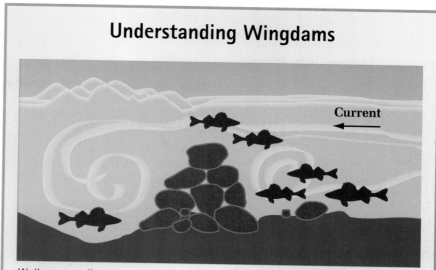

Walleyes usually rest on the flat bottom above a wingdam. They move into the eddy on the front slope of the wingdam or right on top of the wingdam to feed. Walleyes in the eddy below the wingdam are seldom active.

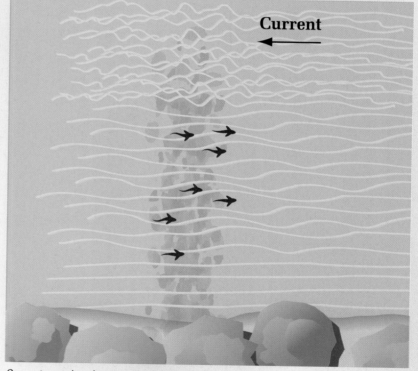

Current speed varies over the length of a wingdam. As a rule, the current is slowest near shore and fastest at the channel end of the wingdam. The fish position themselves where the current is just right.

the current is probably too fast. Most often, strikes will come when the jig is right on top of the wingdam or on the upstream slope. Because of the current, the jig will sink slowly after each twitch, giving walleyes plenty of time to inhale it. Wingdam walleyes are aggressive feeders, so you'll normally feel a very sharp tap, which is your signal to immediately set the hook.

Frequent snags are a big problem in wingdam fishing. Here's a trick that will preserve your jig supply. When you get snagged, simply let out line until it forms a belly downstream of the wingdam. Then jerk the rod sharply. The pressure of the current on the line creates a downstream pull, freeing the jig. This technique works at least 75 percent of the time.

The outfit I use for casting to wingdams is similar to the one I described for vertical jigging, but I like a shorter rod, such as a 5¼ footer with an even faster action; it gives you an unbelievably quick hookset.

Fishing Riprap

Riprap, found in practically all big rivers, consists of rock or pieces of concrete placed along highly erodable sections of the shoreline to stabilize it during high water. Walleyes, being fond of a rocky bottom, are drawn to riprapped banks, especially those in predominately sandy reaches.

Riprap makes good spawning habitat in spring and is a prime feeding area throughout the rest of the open-water season. In spring and fall, you'll often find walleyes holding very tight to the bank, in two to five feet of

water. In summer, they're usually in eight to 12 feet.

The equipment and jigs used for casting to riprap are identical to those used for fishing wingdams. If the current is slow, you can hold your boat within casting distance of the bank, cast perpendicular to it, and work the jig down the slope in the same fashion you would fish a wingdam. Cast as close to shore as possible; the fish will often hit within a few feet of the bank.

If the current is fast, however, it it will catch your line and sweep your jig away before it can reach bottom. In this situation, it's best

Riprap makes ideal walleye cover.

to keep your boat tight to the bank, where the current is much slower. Make downstream casts parallel to the bank and retrieve the jig upstream. If you cast upstream and retrieve downstream, you'll be snagged constantly and you won't be able to use the downstream belly method described earlier to free the jig.

Another productive technique is casting or trolling crankbaits along the riprap. In spring and fall, when the fish are holding tight to the bank, you can cast or long-line an unweighted crankbait parallel to the riprap. In summer, when the fish are deeper, you'll probably need a lead-line rig to get down.

If you haven't tried fishing walleyes in big rivers, you should. River walleyes are a different breed; they're more aggressive than lake walleyes, they fight harder and they're less affected by cold fronts and other weather changes.

The techniques we've described here will get you started right, so you won't have to endure all those expletives from fellow anglers.

Good Riprap vs. Bad Riprap

The best riprap consists of rock or pieces of concrete no more than a foot in diameter. The smaller material probably provides better shelter for baitfish.

Huge concrete slabs or car-size boulders seldom attract many walleyes.

How to Unsnag Your Lure in Current

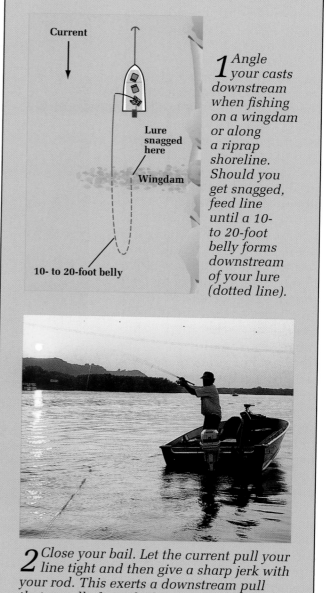

Current

Lure snagged here

Wingdam

10- to 20-foot belly

1 Angle your casts downstream when fishing on a wingdam or along a riprap shoreline. Should you get snagged, feed line until a 10- to 20-foot belly forms downstream of your lure (dotted line).

2 Close your bail. Let the current pull your line tight and then give a sharp jerk with your rod. This exerts a downstream pull that usually frees the bait.

Shallow Thinking for Big Walleyes

Funny thing about walleyes. They're known for their light-sensitive eyes and their habit of hugging the bottom in deep water. You often read that the reason walleyes stay deep is that sunlight "hurts their eyes." So why is it then that practically all of the trophy walleyes I've caught have come out of shallow water—generally from depths of five feet or less?

As we've already discussed, (pp.6-7) it's not that walleyes stay deep because they can't stand the bright light: They can just see better in near-darkness than any of their normal prey species, so they can gain a significant predatory advantage by hanging out in deep water.

But this doesn't mean that walleyes necessarily stay deep all the time. Of all the factors that affect their movement pattern, food is by far the most important. Walleyes go wherever they must to find a meal, and when their food moves into shallow water, so do they. For some reason, big walleyes seem more inclined to feed in the shallows than small ones. Could be that smaller walleyes hesitate to move out of the depths for fear of shallow-water predators, such as northern pike and muskies.

Catching big walleyes in deep water is a tough assignment. They may feed for only a half hour or so each day, moving into their feeding areas around dawn or dusk and sometimes after dark. If you're not at the right place

Plenty of big walleyes come from shallow water.

at the right time with exactly the right bait, you don't stand much of a chance. But walleyes feeding in the shallows are different. They often feed all day long, and you have a much better idea of where they're going to be. Here are some of my favorite shallow-water-walleye situations:

Prairie Reservoirs in Late Fall

Prairie reservoirs, such as North Dakota's Lake Sakakawea and South Dakota's Lake Oahe, are known for their ability to produce trophy walleyes, and they produce them most consistently in fall. Throughout most of the year, walleyes in these lakes relate strongly to the deep water of the old river channel. But in fall, from late September through early November, the fish commonly move out of the river channel and concentrate on rocky points, where they feed on smelt.

These lakes are full of rocky points, but only the ones near the old river channel draw good numbers of walleyes. Fish using these points can easily retreat to the security of deep water when they're not feeding. The best way to find points near deep water is to check a reservoir map. You'll see that

Look for a point where the wind is blowing in, creating a mudline. There, walleyes can feed comfortably in low-light conditions.

the old river channel meanders back and forth across the lake basin. Mark the spots where it swings into shore just off the tip of a point. Ignore the points where the channel follows the opposite side of the basin.

The very best time to fish these points is during an onshore wind. Waves crashing into the shoreline stir up silt, creating a mudline which is your visual clue that conditions are right for a prime walleye bite. The

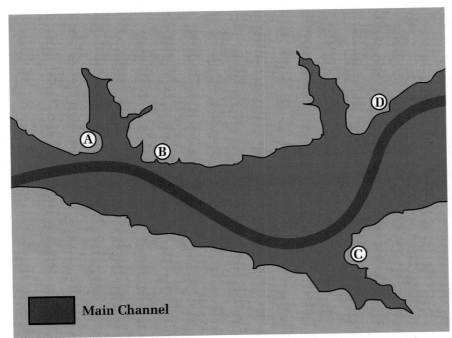

Main Channel

The most productive points (A, B, C and D) are those near the old river channel. Points adjacent to a wide flat are much less likely to hold walleyes.

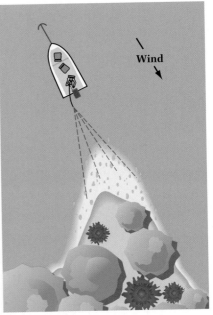

Wind

Anchor just upwind of a point that is holding fish, positioning the boat so you can work the entire shallow shelf.

wind pushes plankton into shore, drawing minnows which, in turn, draw smelt. In the roily water, walleyes do not hesitate to move into depths of two to four feet to feed on the smelt, even in midday.

To locate a productive point, try the "hit-and-run" technique. Pick a likely-looking point on your map, hold just off the tip with your trolling motor, and cast a ⅛- to ¼-ounce jig tipped with a 3- to 5-inch minnow as close to shore as possible. Slowly hop the jig back along the bottom and when it reaches a depth greater than five feet, reel in and cast again. If you work all the way around the point without getting hit, try the next likely point. Once you find a point that is holding fish, drop anchor so you can work it more thoroughly. As long as the wind

is blowing, walleyes keep moving in.

This is probably the best big-walleye pattern I've run across. Daily catches of a

dozen walleyes averaging 8 pounds are not uncommon, and don't be surprised if you haul in an occasional lunker in the 12-pound class.

This trophy struck in shallow flooded timber.

Summer Night Fishing on Canadian Shield Lakes

Despite their deep, cold, infertile water, certain lakes on the Canadian Shield produce good numbers of trophy-caliber walleyes. As a rule, the best shield lakes are those with an abundance of high-fat forage, particularly dwarf ciscoes (p.25).

Because of the deep water in these lakes, they're slow to warm up in spring. In fact, the big walleyes don't really turn on until late June or early July. Then they start gorging themselves on ciscoes. In order to catch walleyes consistently at this time, you must understand the ciscoes' movement pattern.

Ciscoes are coldwater fish, but you can find them along shore and in shallow bays in spring, as long as the water temperature stays below the mid-60s. Once summer sets in, however, they move to deeper water and most of the walleyes follow. But ciscoes have a habit of coming to the surface in the evening to feed on hatching insects; when they do, the walleyes are not far behind.

By far the easiest way to catch these fish is casting or trolling with floating

Shield-lake walleyes love big minnowbaits!

Ciscoes dimpling the water in the evening are a good sign that walleyes will be feeding near the surface once the sun goes down.

minnowbaits. I normally use 5- to 7-inchers, in blue-and-silver or black-and-silver, to match the size and color of the ciscoes.

In midday, when fishing is slow, do a little scouting to find rocky reefs that top out at seven feet or less. When you find one, mark the edges with jugs or buoys that you can easily spot with a light after dark. Try to find and mark several reefs, so you

Mark a likely reef by placing jugs at each end. This way, you can locate it easily after dark without having to run your boat over it and spook the fish.

have some options. Then, starting a half-hour before sunset, motor to within casting distance of a reef. Don't get right on top of it or you'll spook the fish. Cast a minnowbait over the reef and retrieve slowly while using an electric motor to keep your distance. Move around the reef so you can cover it thoroughly. If the walleyes are there, they'll hit right away.

But not all of the walleyes feed over reefs. Ciscoes may find hatching insects most anywhere, and it's not unusual to find walleyes chasing them near the surface over water more than 100 feet deep. When this is happening, try some longline trolling with the same shallow-running minnowbaits. Let out as much as 150 feet of line to minimize

Popular Night-Fishing Lures

Rapala X-Rap

Rapala Minnow Rap

Storm ThunderStick

the chance that you'll spook fish with the boat. For best success, troll over deep water in narrow arms or channels, where the fish are somewhat confined.

Night-fishing on shield lakes is predominately a big-walleye pattern. You may not catch a lot of fish, but your chances of taking 10-pound-plus monsters are excellent.

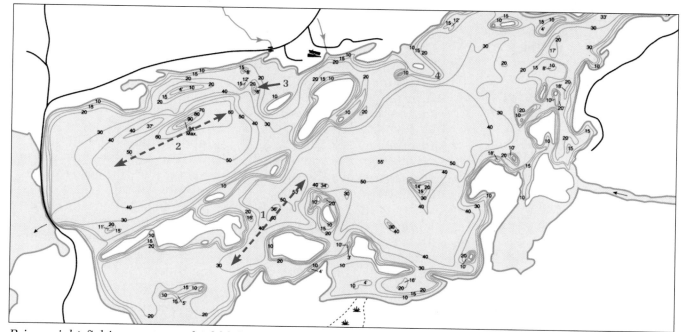

Prime night-fishing spots on shield lakes include (1) a deep channel between islands, (2) over the deepest part of a basin, (3) a shallow reef and (4) the extended lip of a point.

The tailwaters of big-river dams attract walleyes when there's still snow on the ground.

Prespawn Period on Big Rivers

Long before most Northern lakes are ice-free, legions of anglers descend on big rivers that are known to hold good walleye populations. You can find outstanding springtime walleye fishing in dozens of big rivers from Washington state to New York, plus innumerable others in southern Canada.

Die-hard river fishermen begin chasing walleyes as soon as enough ice melts to allow them to slide a boat into the water. On a frigid January day years ago, some buddies and I decided to try a little early-season river fishing, but when we got to the boat landing, it was completely iced in. We were determined to get on the water, so we spent a couple of hours chopping a hole in the ice big enough for the boat. After we got the boat off the trailer, they sat in the bow and rocked back and forth to break ice while I ran the motor. It took more than an hour to clear enough ice so we could start fishing. As I recall, we caught a few dinky walleyes, but we soon got tired of our lines fouling on ice chunks, so we quit.

Since then, I've gained a little sanity. I now wait until the river is ice-free and the warming water starts to activate the big walleyes, drawing them toward the riprap shorelines where they will spawn when the water temperature reaches the upper 40s. The trick is knowing exactly when to be there. If you're too early, the fish are still scattered in deep water, feeding sporadically. If you're too late, they have started to spawn and will refuse to bite. But if you hit it just right—in the week before spawning begins—you'll find the fish tight to the rocky banks, at depths of two to five feet, and feeding as actively as they will all year. The best way to determine the right time is to check the water temperature; it should be in the 43- to 46-degree range.

The ideal spawning site is a riprap bank with a shallow lip, no more than 10 feet deep, that extends well out into the river before dropping into deep water. Such a lip gives the walleyes a relatively flat surface where they can mill about and deposit their eggs. Seldom will you find spawners along a bank that plunges straight into the depths.

The fish prefer a light current, maybe 1 to 2 mph, to keep silt from accumulating on the eggs and smothering them. You'll rarely find them in completely slack water or in fast current. In most big rivers, early spring currents easily exceed the 2 mph mark, so you'll have to

find eddies where the current is slower. Luckily, that's not much of a problem; most any point or sharp bend in the river has an eddy downstream of it.

Once you find a spot that is holding fish, engrave it in your memory and check it every time you go out. Walleyes have a strong homing tendency and will return to the same spawning sites year after year.

For taking prespawn walleyes on shallow riprap, it's tough to beat curlytail jigs. I usually start with a ⅛-ounce chartreuse or chartreuse-and-orange jig head, tipped with a 3-inch chartreuse tail. Although most anglers insist on tipping their jigs with minnows, it's really not necessary because the fish are on such a feeding binge. If the wind or current keeps you from getting to the bottom with a ⅛-ounce head, try a ¼-ounce.

I like to anchor at the head of an eddy and angle my casts downstream so they land within inches of the bank. Then I work the jig back upstream with the shortest possible twitches, followed by pauses. When the fish are really "on," most hits will come within a few feet of the bank; when fishing is slower, you may have to work the jig into seven or eight feet of water. You shouldn't have any trouble detecting strikes; walleyes crack the jig as it is sinking.

After working a stretch of riprap thoroughly, lift anchor, slide downstream a little and work another stretch. I feel I can work an area much more thoroughly by anchoring than by attempting to hold my position with a trolling motor.

Like the other techniques I've mentioned, this is definitely a big-fish method. You're fishing mainly for prespawn females, so it's unusual to take anything under 4 pounds, and I've had days when all of the fish ran 6 to 11 pounds.

There's a simple reason why such a high percentage of trophy-class walleyes come from shallow water: When big walleyes are shallow, they're almost always feeding aggressively. If you're intent on catching the fish of a lifetime, that sure makes your job a lot easier.

Where to Find Prespawn Walleyes

A riprap bank that has plenty of small rock and an extended lip makes an ideal spot for walleyes to spawn. Prespawn females move into these areas several days before spawning begins.

Look for eddies that form downstream of points or sharp bends in the river channel. Walleyes working their way upriver to spawn rest in these slackwater areas where they do not have to fight the current.

BREAK THE RULES FOR VIRGIN-WATER WALLEYES

"We're headin' out to the reef," yelled Jim Corbett as he cranked up the 10-horse motor. "We'll see you out there, eh?" As he and Mark Hanson pulled away from shore, I caught a glimpse of a big red-and-white Dardevle hanging from his rod. "Does he think he's gonna catch walleyes on that?" I asked my fishing partner, Mike Sheehan. Mike just shook his head and chuckled.

We were only minutes behind them, but when we pulled up to the reef, both were fighting fish. "Four walleyes in about two minutes," Jim crowed as we approached their boat. "Not too bad, eh?"

Who says a walleye won't hit a big Dardevle?

Corbett, a rugged, good-natured Canadian, owned "Trophy Fish Outposts" of Pickle Lake, Ontario. He had operated fishing camps most of his life, but became frustrated by the declining quality of walleye fishing throughout that region of Ontario. "Most of the lakes are just getting fished too hard," Corbett said. "I wanted to take my customers into lakes that were untouched, so I approached the Fort Hope Band of Ojibway and negotiated a special deal that allows me to operate fishing camps on several lakes on their lands—lakes that have hardly ever been fished."

Hanson, Sheehan and I had come to fish Machawaian Lake, one of Corbett's newly opened waters. Only one party had been into the camp before us, so most of the lake had not been thoroughly explored. When Corbett told us he was heading out to fish "the reef," he didn't mean it was the lake's only reef, it was just the only one he knew about.

I had fished many remote walleye lakes before, but this one was different. It wasn't just a lightly fished lake, it was a lake that had not seen any significant fishing pressure for many years. I'm sure that the vast majority of walleyes in the lake had never seen an angler's bait.

That may explain why the fish struck Dardevles or

practically any bait we threw at them. And the type of retrieve didn't seem to matter much either. Sometimes we "ripped" the baits; other

times we worked them slowly. But the walleyes' taste in lures and presentation wasn't the only strange behavior I observed. Over the next few days, I saw them doing things I've never seen them doing in other lakes, even in remote lakes that see only a few anglers each season. They evidently hadn't read "the book" on feeding locations and feeding times either.

Presentation

Not knowing what to expect on Machawaian, we brought so much gear that two float plane flights were needed to carry it all in from nearby Fort Hope. When Corbett saw all the tackle, plus a flat of nightcrawlers and 5 pounds of leeches, he started to laugh. "You won't need any of that stuff," he promised. "These fish haven't been educated, eh?"

No kidding! Walleyes that eat Dardevles like candy?

Maybe they've been crossbreeding with northern pike. Or maybe they just haven't seen enough lures to develop a rating system. Whatever the reason, these walleyes seemed to like the big spoons about as well as anything. But being a jig-fishing addict, I opted for that method.

We were fishing water from two to seven feet deep, so I tied on a ⅛-ounce jighead tipped with a 3-inch curly-tail grub, a combination that would sink slowly but still

get down to the bottom—just what the book says you need under those conditions. The slow sink rate supposedly gives walleyes a longer look at the jig, increasing the odds that they will strike.

But Corbett evidently hadn't read the book. On the afternoon I fished with him, he tossed a clunky jig weighing at least ¾ ounce and caught just as many walleyes as I did. The paint was all chipped off his jig, but it didn't seem to matter. At one

How to Make a Backcountry Depthfinder/Navigation Setup

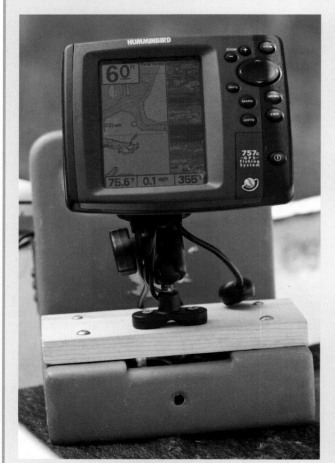

1 Rig a combination depth finder/GPS unit on a "blue box" designed for ice fishing. Mount the module on the handle of the box using a hose clamp. A motorcycle or gel-cel battery provides the power. This setup will not only help you locate fish and return to productive spots, it allows you to explore remote areas without fear of getting lost.

2 Attach your transducer to a 1x4 board. Be sure the transducer's face is tilted so it catches water when the boat is moving.

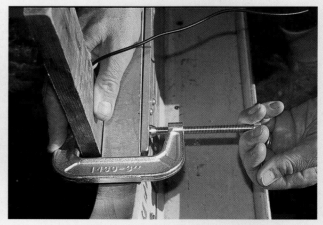

3 C-clamp the board to your transom to hold it in place. The face of the transducer should be just a little below the bottom of the boat.

Lures for Backcountry Walleyes

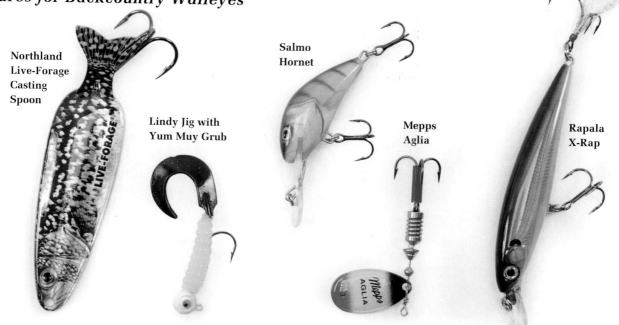

Northland Live-Forage Casting Spoon

Lindy Jig with Yum Muy Grub

Salmo Hornet

Mepps Aglia

Rapala X-Rap

point he removed the curly-tail, leaving only the plain lead head. "Let's see if they'll hit that, eh?" he chuckled. I have to admit that I was a little surprised when his first and second cast each produced a fish. Not only did the sink-rate rule go by the boards, color and action didn't matter much either. These fish attacked anything that moved.

Over the course of the trip, we also had good success on a variety of other lures including minnowbaits, crankbaits and in-line spinners.

Another puzzling phenomenon: Unlike walleyes in most clear-water lakes, Machawaian Lake walleyes weren't a bit line-shy. While the rest of us were using low-vis 6-pound mono, Corbett was working his magic using 12-pound mono and a 40-pound wire leader.

And then there's the outboard motor issue. Everyone knows that you can't run an outboard over walleyes in shallow water without spooking them. Yet, that's exactly what we did most of the time on Machawaian, because we didn't have an electric trolling motor. Evidently, line-shyness and aversion to the sound of an outboard are not inborn traits, but behaviors that develop as a response to fishing pressure.

Locations & Times

We had sunny weather for the majority of our trip, yet we consistently caught walleyes in two or three feet of water on top of rocky reefs, even in the middle of the day. On some reefs, you could actually see the walleye schools. When we saw them, we just backed the boat off a bit, cast to them with curlytail jigs and caught them one after another.

Machawaian Lake has clear water with only a light bog stain; you can easily see the bottom in eight feet. In a heavily fished lake with water that clear, you'd seldom find walleyes in less than 15 feet under the same conditions. Makes you wonder—do walleyes really retreat to the depths to avoid sunlight? Or do they hide out in deep water for some other reason? Could be that the tendency to go deep evolved as a survival mechanism; maybe the walleyes that were visible in clear, shallow water ended up in the frying pan.

The sound of an outboard doesn't seem to bother virgin-water walleyes.

Good-sized inlet streams draw huge numbers of walleyes throughout the open-water season. The flowing water concentrates food which, in turn, attracts walleyes.

Weedy bays that seem more like pike habitat are often prime walleye producers. Again, walleyes go where the food is.

We know that walleyes tend to feed most heavily on the windward side of a lake, where wave action concentrates plankton, draws in baitfish and reduces water clarity. But in Machawaian, it really didn't matter what side of the lake you were on. The fish bit like crazy in the rough water, but they bit well in the calm water, too. We caught hundreds of walleyes along sheltered shorelines, in protected bays and on shallow reefs where the water was perfectly flat. Again, maybe all the talk about needing "a good walleye chop" is related more to fishing pressure than to food availability or reduced water clarity.

Another "known fact" is that walleyes like a hard bottom. In Machawaian, almost every shallow, rocky reef was loaded with walleyes, but most of the bigger walleyes were taken in bays and along weedy shorelines where the bottom was soft. Could it be that the walleye population in Machawaian is so large that there just isn't enough feeding space on the reefs? Or—maybe the bigger walleyes don't like competing with hordes of smaller ones, so they opt to forage in secondary feeding zones.

If there ever was a "universal rule" in walleye fishing, it would be that walleyes in clear lakes feed most heavily in dim-light periods—around dawn and dusk or after dark. But if you planned your Machawaian Lake fishing schedule around that rule, you'd be making a big mistake. As far as I could tell, time of day was irrelevant. If there was any time-related pattern, it was just the opposite of the rule. Fishing in midday was a little

Many remote walleye lakes do not have accurate hydrographic maps, but you can locate likely spots by flying over the lake with an airplane and noting the location of reefs, extended points, weedy bays and other potential walleye haunts.

better than under dim-light conditions.

When you witness all this strange walleye behavior first-hand, it makes you wonder about the validity of the walleye-fishing rules we've come to accept as gospel. It also helps explain why following the rules doesn't always put more walleyes in the boat. Most anglers tend to be too rigid in planning their walleye-fishing strategy.

Willingness to break the rules is what separates the real pros from the rest of the walleye-fishing crowd.

Walleyes tend to follow the rules more closely in heavily fished waters, and the rules have some relevance even on remote waters that see only light fishing pressure. But if you ever have a chance to do some walleye fishing on "virgin" waters like Machawaian, don't bother to pack that rule book.

How to Make a Wire Leader

Make a jig-fishing leader from an 8-inch piece of single-strand (about 30-pound test) wire. Using haywire twists, attach a small barrel swivel to one end and the jig to the other end (below).

The wire leader prevents pike bite-offs (left) and won't reduce the number of walleye strikes.

RUNNIN' AND GUNNIN' FOR WINTER WALLEYES

After staring at a pair of motionless tip-ups all afternoon, I was just getting ready to wind them in when I spotted Jim Schneider's pick-up heading my way. He pulled right up to me, rolled down the window and asked, "Did ya leave any for me?"

"This spot's dead," I informed him. "Caught a couple walleyes first thing this morning and haven't had a flag since."

Paying no attention to the bad news, he started unloading his fishing gear as I was winding in one of my tips-ups. "Mind if I use your hole?" he inquired. "It's all yours," I said. "I'm outta here."

Before I could get my other tip-up wound in, Jim set the hook and soon had a nice walleye flopping on the ice.

"Waddya think of these baits?" he smirked, displaying the little minnow-shaped lure with a plastic tail and bent-up hooks on either end. "It's a Jigging Rap."

I was speechless. After I'd bombed out in that hole for more than six hours with a tip-up and lively minnow, he catches a walleye within seconds on a chunk of painted lead? To add to the embarrassment, he proceeded to ice two more nice walleyes while I was standing there.

If my memory serves me correctly, that incident took place back in 1968. Since then, I've never gone ice fishing without a good supply of Jigging Raps.

After that eye-opening experience, I started to take jigging a lot more seriously. I began playing around with other types of jigging baits, including a variety of blade-baits and jigging spoons.

I spent a lot of time trying to figure out exactly how and when to use each of these bait types, but once I started getting proficient with them, my walleye catch rate sky-rocketed. I was catching two or three times as many walleyes as I used to catch on tip-ups alone.

There are two main reasons why jigging is so effective:

- The jigging action draws strikes from walleyes that ignore a stationary bait.
- Jigging enables you to be highly mobile. When you're fishing with a tip-up or a float rig, you have to readjust your depth every time you move. With a jigging lure, all you do is reel up and drop your line down another hole.

Portable ice shelters with a flip-up top make it easy to change locations quickly. When the weather is nice, flip back the top and you have a combination seat/windbreak.

To catch walleyes like this, keep moving and stay away from the crowd!

pointers for using this gear to your best advantage:

Electronics

A handheld GPS unit is one of your most important ice-fishing tools, especially if you remembered to punch in some of your favorite summertime spots. A GPS, especially one that can be loaded with detailed hydrographic maps, will save you hours of search time.

Another time saver is a handheld, flash-light-type sounder. Unless you're on slush-ice, you should be able to squirt a little water on the ice and get depth read-ings without taking time to drill holes.

Most serious wall-eye anglers use a sensitive flasher, such as a Vexilar FL-20, which enables them to see their lure and the fish. This way, they can see how the fish respond to different jigging actions.

Auger

A lightweight, fast-cutting power auger, like the Strikemaster Laser, is a must for maximum mobility. If you have to lug a heavy auger and struggle to cut each hole, you won't cover much territory.

After you've determined the configuration of the structure using your handheld sounder, drill rows of holes at various depths around the entire perimeter of the structure (below). Be sure

How to Jig for Winter Walleyes

Although tip-ups and float rigs remain effective, jigging has become the primary technique of serious winter walleye anglers. In years past, most fishermen sat in a fish house and waited for the walleyes to come to them. Now anglers drill dozens of holes along structure; they fish in one hole for a few minutes and then jump to the next.

But to be successful with this "run-and-gun" tech-nique, you've got to have the right equipment and know what to do with it. Here are some equipment recommen-dations, along with a few

What to Look for in a Jigging Rod

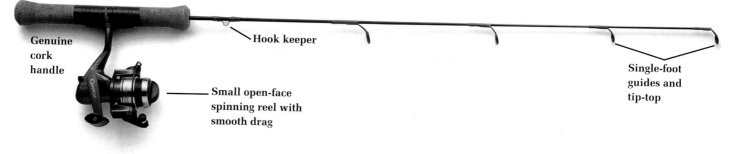

Genuine cork handle

Hook keeper

Small open-face spinning reel with smooth drag

Single-foot guides and tip-top

to follow the contour of any points or inside turns; these spots are likely to hold the most walleyes.

The deepest holes are likely to be best in midday. But starting at dusk, the shallower holes will come to life.

Try to get all your holes drilled before dusk; if you start drilling late in the day, when the fish are coming in to feed, you'll drive them away and they may not come back.

Rod and Reel

For most of my winter walleye jigging, I use a fairly stiff graphite rod (about 30 inches long) and a light spinning reel spooled with limp 6-pound-test mono. A single-foot tip-top and guides will minimize ice build-up. If your rod has a standard tip-top, replace it with a good-sized fly rod tip-top.

Terminal Tackle

Attach a small, round-nosed clip to the end of your line so you can change baits quickly. It's a lot easier than trying to tie knots with cold fingers.

Line twist is a big problem when fishing with jigging baits. The solution is to splice a small barrel swivel (size 12) into the line about 18 inches above the lure.

Jigging Tips

There's a lot more to jigging for winter walleyes than dropping your bait down the hole and jerking it up and down.

The first challenge is to select the right type and color lure for the water you're fishing.

In clear water, I generally use a jigging spoon or swimming minnow, usually in natural baitfish colors such as silver, silver-and-green, gold or perch.

In murky water, I've had my best luck with a swimming minnow or bladebait in bright or fluorescent colors, particularly chartreuse-and-orange.

The next challenge is to develop the right jigging stroke. Here are some tips for using each type of bait:

Swimming Minnow. This bait darts forward with an upward sweep of the rod.

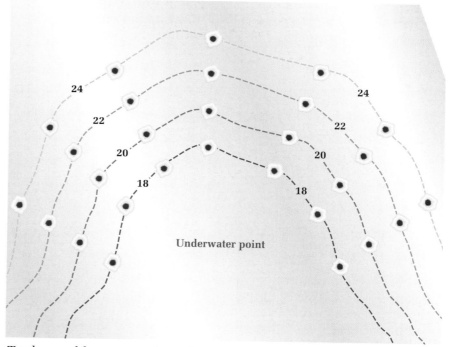

Underwater point

To thoroughly cover a piece of structure, such as a point, drill rows of holes around the contours at 2-foot intervals. If the structure tops out at 18 feet, for instance, and then gradually slopes down to 24, drill four rows of holes at 2-foot intervals to cover the entire drop-off.

Jigging Baits for Winter Walleyes

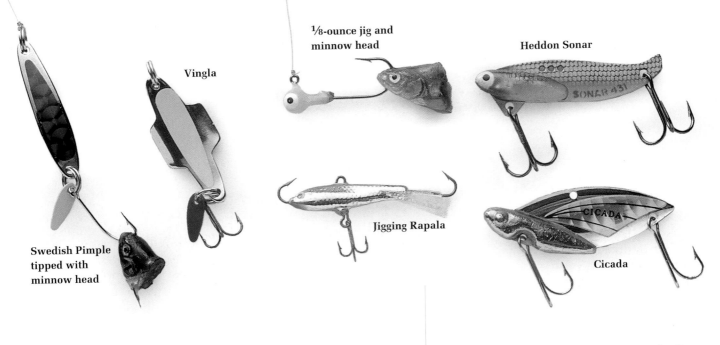

Vingla

⅛-ounce jig and minnow head

Heddon Sonar

Swedish Pimple tipped with minnow head

Jigging Rapala

Cicada

Each sweep sends the bait darting off in a slightly different direction, so you will eventually cover a good-sized circle surrounding your hole.

After each sweep, hold your rod motionless while the bait settles back to center; you can tell by watching the angle of the line in your hole. Try to keep the bait 6 to 12 inches off the bottom.

The strike will usually come several seconds after the bait has settled. If you jig the bait non-stop, without hesitating between strokes, you'll get far fewer strikes.

Jigging Spoon. Instead of darting to the side on the upward sweep, this bait flutters to the side as it sinks on a slack line. The wider and thinner the spoon, the farther to the side it glides.

If you make the mistake of lowering the bait on a taut

Tipping Tips

Tip a swimming minnow by adding a perch eye (where legal) or minnow head to the treble hook on the underside. It's a good idea to replace the standard treble with a larger one if you plan on tipping.

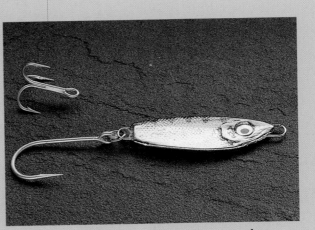

Before tipping a jigging spoon, remove the treble hook and add a single hook with an eye large enough to slip over the split-ring. A single hook improves your hooking percentage because the bait doesn't fill the hook gap.

line, you'll kill the sideways action and the bait will not be as effective.

When walleyes are aggressive, they'll sometimes strike a jigging spoon as it is sinking; but more often, they'll grab it after it settles. So it's important that you hesitate several seconds between jigging strokes, just as you would with a swimming minnow.

Bladebait. This bait doesn't dart or flutter to the side, but it emits a strong vibration on the upward sweep, explaining why it's so effective in low-clarity water.

Most often, a walleye strikes a bladebait as it is sinking, so the best technique is to give the bait a sharp upward sweep, and then follow it down with your rodtip to keep the line taut.

Rather than use a short jigging rod, some bladebait anglers opt for a standard-length spinning rod. They prefer to stand next to the hole and work the bait with longer upward sweeps.

Whatever rod you prefer, establish a regular jigging pattern, without long pauses between the sweeps. If you feel a tap or bump as the bait is sinking, or if it just doesn't sink the way it should, set the hook.

With any of the baits, your odds are best on the first few jigging strokes in a given hole. Walleyes tend to "wise up" to the bait after a short while so, unless the fish are moving, I seldom work the same hole for more than five minutes.

There's no arguing the fact that runnin' and gunnin' is a lot of work. But then again there's no better way to put a mess of walleyes on the ice.

Flasher Tips

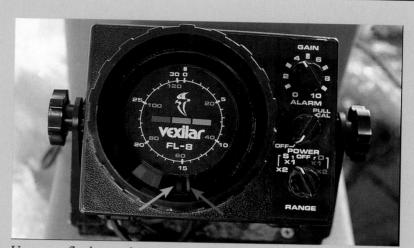

Use your flasher to fine-tune your jigging presentation. When a walleye appears on the dial (red arrow), try giving the bait (green arrow) a sharp twitch. If the fish moves away and doesn't return, try a softer twitch next time or try teasing the fish by pulling the bait upward while jigging it lightly. Keep experimenting until you find the action that makes the fish strike.

Most modern flasher units come as a package, complete with a carrying case, battery and battery indicator. Many units also have dual-beam transducers that let you change the cone angle from 9 to 12 degrees. Choose 12 degrees for shallow water, 9 degrees for deep.

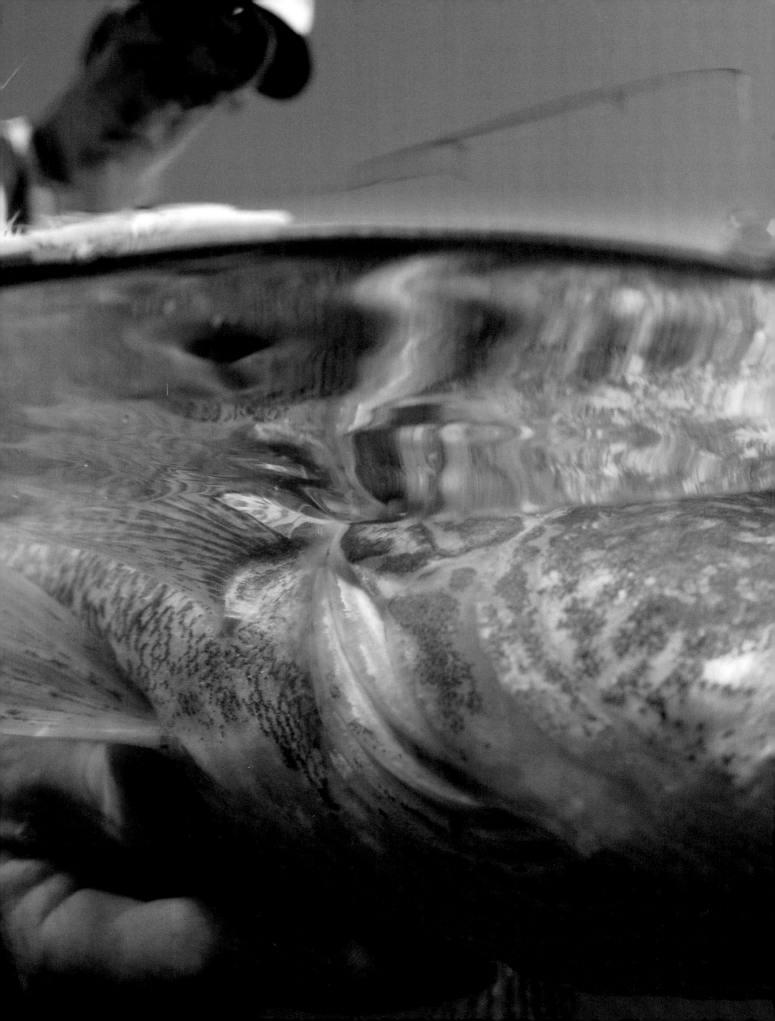

WHEN THE GOING GETS TOUGH

When the bite is off, you'll have to dig deep into your bag of tricks to put some walleyes in the boat.

Rx for Common Walleye Headaches

I've got a buddy who always wears his "Fisherman's Excuse Cap" when we go walleye fishing. The whole thing is plastered with every conceivable reason why the fish aren't biting: "It's too windy," "It's too sunny," "The water's too muddy," etc.

Whenever the fish aren't cooperating, he always looks at his cap to find an excuse that suits the situation. To tell you the truth, I'm getting a little tired of his antics.

If you're a serious walleye angler, you really don't need an excuse hat. What you do need are some solutions. On the pages that follow are some of the most common walleye-fishing headaches and some proven remedies.

Cold-front walleyes may be so dormant that divers can swim up and touch them.

Cold Fronts

Most anglers believe that walleyes go much deeper and refuse to bite under cold-front conditions, but that is seldom the case. As a rule, you'll find them in pretty much the same places where they were before the front. They're just not as active.

Often the sky becomes very clear after the front passes, and the increased light penetration drives the fish a little deeper. But they're just as likely to go shallower, burying themselves in the weeds.

Here are some tips for cold-front walleyes:

Slower & Smaller

A slow, tantalizing retrieve definitely draws more strikes, but slowing down may not be easy unless you downsize your baits and use lighter sinkers. With a 1/16-ounce jig, for instance, you're forced to retrieve more slowly than you would with a 1/8-ounce; otherwise, you couldn't keep it on the bottom.

A Sensitive Touch

Even under the toughest cold-front conditions, live bait such as minnows, leeches or nightcrawlers will usually tempt a few fish to bite. But the fish are not aggressive and, if your rod is not sensitive enough, you won't feel the pick-up. By the time you realize you have a bite, the fish has already dropped the bait.

You may flinch at the price of some of an ultra-sensitive graphite rod but, when you're dealing with finicky cold-front walleyes, that equipment is well worth the money.

Stinger Hooks

Cold-front walleyes are notorious short-strikers. To solve the problem, jig-and-minnow fishermen commonly add a stinger hook; this way, when a walleye takes a half-hearted nip at the minnow's tail, it gets hooked.

But stingers are not just for a jig and minnow. They can be used on a jig tipped with other kinds of live bait, as well as with soft-plastic, hair or feather dressings. Just tie a small treble hook onto the

The clear-out after a cold front makes for a walleye fishing challenge.

Add a stinger by tying a length of stiff 12- to 15-pound line, to the bend of your hook and then adding a size 12 or 14 treble hook (top). Use just enough mono so the treble extends to the bait's tail. Or, just use a jig with a clip-on stinger (bottom).

bend of the jig hook as shown above. The stiff line will hold the lightweight treble alongside the tail while the bait swims normally. If you're using a clip-on stinger, allow that to swing freely as well.

You can also tie a stinger to the bend of a floating jig head or a plain live-bait hook.

Slip-bobber Fishing

Even if walleyes aren't feeding, you can tempt a few bites by dangling a squirming leech or other live bait from a slip-bobber rig. One well-known walleye guide told me why slip-bobber rigs work so well. "It's like setting a donut out on the kitchen table," he chuckled. "You'll walk past it and look at it maybe half-a-dozen times during the day, but eventually you'll pick it up and take a bite."

Night Fishing

If you can't seem to get cold-front walleyes to bite during the day, try fishing at night. I've seen some excellent night bites following days when I boated only a walleye or two. My most productive technique has been still-fishing with a lighted slip-bobber and a leech.

Thunderstorms

A severe thunderstorm is one of nature's most violent events, so it's not surprising that activity patterns of walleye and other fish change dramatically following a major "thunderboomer."

Most expert walleye anglers stay home for a day or two following a bad storm, but if you're intent on fighting the odds, here are some things to try:

Fish Deeper

It's not uncommon for walleyes to go on a major feeding binge when a big, black cloud is approaching. I once caught a dozen 5- to 8-pound walleyes on my favorite lake in the hour before a severe thunderstorm struck. Next day, I returned to the same

Night-Fishing Tips

A lighted slip-bobber makes it easy to detect bites after dark.

Rig your boat with a strong interior light that operates off your boat's 12-volt power system. A good headlamp is also a must for rigging, baiting up and unhooking fish after dark.

Walleyes usually turn on as a thunderstorm is approaching. But heavy thunder and lightning slow the action, sometimes for a couple days.

spot only to find that the walleyes, which previously had been in about 18 feet of water, were gone. But some 2- to 4-pound smallmouth bass, which normally inhabited water five to 10 feet deep, had moved in and were biting like mad.

Reasoning that if the bass were deeper than normal, the walleyes might also be deeper, I moved out to 35 feet. My hunch was right;

within 45 minutes, I boated half a dozen nice walleyes.

Slower & Smaller

Just as downsizing your baits and slowing your retrieve helps catch walleye under cold-front conditions, these techniques can also make a big difference in convincing skittish walleyes to bite following a severe thunderstorm. Night-fishing is worth a try as well.

Fluctuating Water

Always a problem for river fishermen, changing water levels mean trouble for reservoir anglers too. Walleyes and most other gamefish respond instinctively when levels change. When it drops, they go deeper; when it rises, they move shallower. Even a change of only an inch or two makes a big difference.

How & Where to Fish in Rising vs. Falling Water

Rising Water. *Baitfish move into shore to feed on tiny insects they find among the flooded grass and brush, and the walleyes are close behind. Tie on an in-line spinner, ⅛-ounce jig or shallow-running crankbait and try casting right up to shore.*

Falling Water. *When the water starts to drop, walleyes clear out immediately, an instinctive reaction that prevents them from being stranded in an isolated pool. Use a ¼-ounce jig, a deep-diving crankbait or live bait on a slip-sinker rig, and work water 5 to 15 feet deeper than normal.*

Here are some tips for dealing with fluctuating water levels:

Gin-Clear Water

One of my favorite walleye lakes has been getting progressively clearer over the years, probably because of improvements in septic systems. Years ago, when the water clarity was about 5 feet, you could always catch walleyes in midday, even in the hottest, sunniest weather.

Now the clarity is more than 10 feet, and the pattern is much different. Here's how to combat the clear-water problem:

Fish Early or Late

As a rule, it pays to do most of your fishing around dawn or dusk or—better yet—at night. Walleyes feed very little in midday, unless skies are overcast or the water is choppy.

A friend and I recently spent several days fishing a clear Canadian Shield lake during a period of extremely calm, clear weather. Daytime fishing was slow, but we caught several 9- to 11-pound walleyes by casting crankbaits and minnowbaits over shallow reefs after dark.

Play the Wind

If one side of the lake is calm and the other windswept, your chances would be much better on the windy side.

When the water is rising, you'll often find walleyes feeding heavily in brushy cover where the water is less than a foot deep.

The subtle wobble and long profile of a minnowbait make it one of the best walleye producers in ultra-clear lakes.

The wave action causes light rays to scatter when they strike the surface. With the lower light level, walleyes move shallower and start to feed. Wave action also stirs up the bottom, reducing light penetration even more. And the wind blows in plankton, attracting minnows which, in turn, attract walleyes.

Lighter Line

Walleyes in clear lakes tend to be line-shy, so switching to a smaller diameter, less visible line can make a big difference. I'll go as light as 4-pound test, but I make sure my drag is set light enough to avoid breaking off on the hookset. It helps to use a rod with a soft tip to absorb some of the shock.

Fish Deep

If there is adequate oxygen in the depths, walleyes in clear-water lakes will go surprisingly deep, especially in calm, sunny weather. I've caught them as deep as 55 feet and I've heard of guys hauling them out of 70.

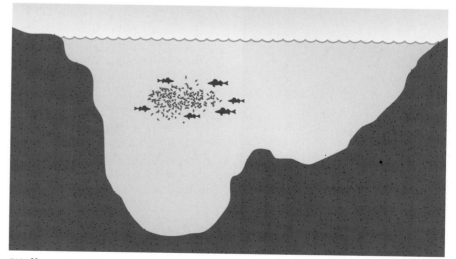

Walleyes in ultra-clear lakes commonly suspend to feed on ciscoes or other pelagic forage fish. It is not unusual to find them over the deepest part of the lake.

For murky-water walleyes, don't hesitate to cast right up to shore.

A jig like this can be snaked through dense weeds.

Check the Weeds

If a lake has heavy weed growth, sunny weather often drives walleyes shallower, not deeper. They bury themselves in cabbage beds or other vegetation that affords them shade. You can still catch them by working a weedless jig tipped with a minnow, leech or 'crawler right through the weeds. Or, work a jig or live-bait rig tight to the weedline.

Look for Suspended Fish

Many clear-water lakes have good populations of pelagic forage, such as ciscoes. Walleyes roam the open water because that's where the food is. You'll often find schools of suspended walleyes over the deepest part of the lake.

To determine which areas are holding walleyes, cover as much water as you can by trolling crankbaits. As you troll, carefully watch your graph, noting the depth of the baitfish and the walleyes. Then select a crankbait that will run at that depth.

Murky Water

A lake with a heavy algae bloom, muddy water or water containing any substance that prevents light from penetrating poses the opposite problem as a gin-clear lake. Because sunlight cannot penetrate, walleyes live in a dark environment all of the time, so feeding is often scattered throughout the day rather than being heaviest at dawn and dusk.

Walleyes may bite at intervals throughout the day, but there are no major feeding peaks. In fact, your chances may actually be better at midday than in morning or evening hours since the direct rays of the sun penetrate enough around high noon to enable fish to better see their prey.

Conversely, increasing cloud cover or wave action can slow the action in murky water. The clouds or choppy surface may reduce light penetration to the point where walleyes can't see well enough to feed.

Here are a few suggestions for tackling the murky water challenge:

Fish Shallow

Walleyes in murky waters often feed close to shore at depths of only two to five feet. Under these conditions, I've had my best success by casting small jigs, in-line spinners or spin-rigs tipped with live bait to within a foot of shore and slowly working them out.

Use a Vibrating Plug

Lures like a Rattlin' Rap, Cordell Spot or Rat-L-Trap sometimes work magic in muddy or otherwise discolored waters. Walleyes have

the ability to detect vibration using their lateral-line sensory system, so they don't have to see the bait.

Try Fluorescent Colors

No matter if you're fishing with leadhead jigs, floating jig heads, spinners or vibrating plugs, fluorescent colors are likely to outproduce standard colors by a wide margin in discolored water.

In extremely murky water, use luminescent (glow-in-the-dark) lures. But don't use lures that glow too brightly. They may spook the fish, probably because they look unnatural.

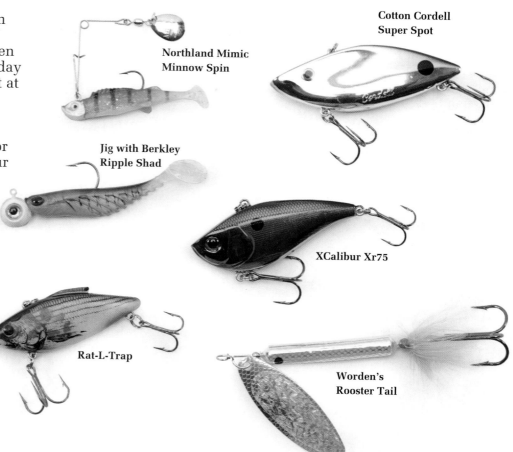

Popular Baits for Murky-Water Walleyes

Northland Mimic Minnow Spin

Cotton Cordell Super Spot

Jig with Berkley Ripple Shad

XCalibur Xr75

Rat-L-Trap

Worden's Rooster Tail

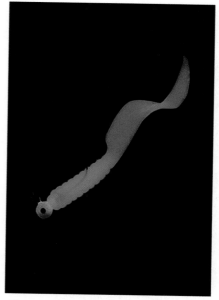

Choose a luminescent bait with a subtle glow.

No Fish-Holding Structure

Even though a lake is teeming with walleyes, you'll have a hard time finding them if there is a lack of structure that concentrates the fish.

The worst possible lake to fish is one with a dishpan basin. There, walleyes have absolutely nothing to associate with, so they can be found almost anywhere.

Here are a few tips to improve your odds under these difficult conditions:

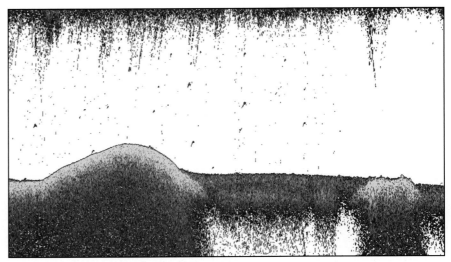

The solid yellow line at the top of this reef indicates a harder bottom; the fuzzy reddish band along the break shows a soft bottom.

Find Hard Bottom

Even though there are no obvious humps, drop-offs or points, there is likely to be some change in the bottom composition. If you can find a patch of gravel or rubble, for example, in a basin that is otherwise all muck or silt, chances are you've located the walleye hangout.

Try Trolling or Casting

In a featureless lake, the more water you cover, the better your chances of putting your bait in front of a fish. That's why trolling or casting with crankbaits is so popular.

When trolling in a dishpan lake, keep a close eye on your depthfinder for schools of fish suspended off the bottom. Food organisms are not necessarily associated with the bottom in lakes of this type, and walleyes do not hesitate to suspend at the depth where prey is most abundant.

If you locate a school of walleyes, be sure to mark the spot carefully for future reference. The fish may be relating to a gravel patch or some other feature that is not apparent to you.

If the fish are tightly concentrated, as is often the case, the best technique may be slip-bobber fishing at the appropriate depth using a lively leech for bait.

Forage Glut

The forage crop fluctuates tremendously in a given body of water. And fishing success is often more closely related to forage abundance than to walleye abundance. A lake

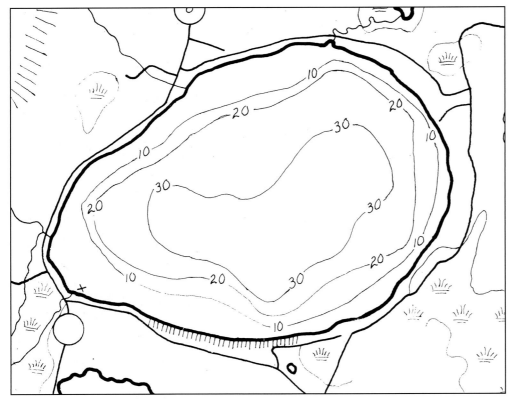

In a featureless basin like this, walleyes can be almost anywhere.

When hordes of bite-sized forage are available, it's not surprising that walleyes won't cooperate.

When you locate a school of walleyes in a dishpan lake, toss out a marker so you don't lose them. Then anchor just upwind and toss out a slip-bobber rig.

can have a tremendous walleye population but, when the food supply is peaking, you'd swear the lake was fished out.

For example, when spring spawning conditions in natural lakes are right, yellow perch have the capacity to get off an enormous hatch that keeps walleyes well-fed for the rest of the year. In midsummer, I've seen schools of perch that actually black out my graph, filling the entire water column from top to bottom. It's no wonder that walleyes aren't too excited about biting.

In big rivers and reservoirs, baitfish like gizzard shad

have boom and bust years, depending mainly on springtime water levels.

A huge forage crop may be the toughest fishing problem of all to crack, but there are a few techniques that can improve your chances:

Fish at Sunrise

Walleyes have to eat sometime during the day. When forage is plentiful, their feeding periods are shorter. In these situations, I've noticed that walleyes often feed for a half-hour or so at sunrise and then turn off for the rest of the day. If you're a late riser, you'll miss the action.

For speed trolling, use a stiff rod that won't bend too much at speeds of 4-plus miles per hour. Attach your bait to a three-way rig with a 3- to 4-ounce sinker (inset).

Speed Trolling

A full-bellied walleye will ignore a minnow, leech or nightcrawler dragged slowly past it, but speed trolling with a crankbait or vibrating plug will sometimes trigger a "reaction" strike.

Jigging

Even when walleyes aren't in a feeding mood, you can often entice a few of then to bite by vertical jigging. They evidently become curious when they see a jig being bounced up and down off the bottom. Then, a playful "nip" can be a big mistake.

Rip-jigging (p.91) is also a proven technique for triggering full-bellied walleyes to strike.

Spinner Fishing

The flash and thump of a spinner blade often has a near-magical effect on well-fed walleyes. On dozens of occasions, I've seen the fish pay no attention to a plain live-bait rig, but aggressively take the same rig after a small spinner blade was added.

Popular Speed-Trolling Baits

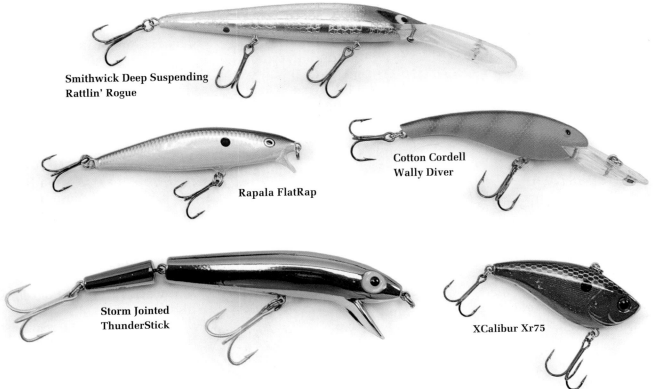

Smithwick Deep Suspending Rattlin' Rogue

Rapala FlatRap

Cotton Cordell Wally Diver

Storm Jointed ThunderStick

XCalibur Xr75

Boat Traffic

Walleye pros know that the worst time to go fishing is on opening day, when lakes are overrun with anglers. If there's too much commotion, the fish simply won't feed.

Weekend and holiday anglers are plagued by speedboats, waterskiers and jet skis. The best way to solve the boat-traffic problem is to avoid it by getting out early in the morning, before the boating crowd gets out of bed. Evening fishing is not as good. Even after the traffic subsides, it may be several hours before the fish settle down and start feeding.

But if you must fish in a high-traffic situation, here are a few techniques to try:

Speed Trolling

Just as this technique draws reaction strikes during a baitfish glut, it may also draw the attention of walleyes that have been "put down" by incessant boat traffic.

Fish Deeper

Walleyes that normally cruise shallow water move much deeper when waves from the boats start crashing into the shoreline. If the walleyes are normally in 10 feet of water, don't be afraid to try 20.

Sometimes the Walleyes Win

You can greatly improve your walleye-fishing success by applying the techniques we've described, but there will be times when nothing you do seems to work.

Consider what once happened at the South Dakota Governor's Cup Walleye Tournament, a prestigious

It's possible to catch walleyes in high-traffic situations, but you'll have to do everything just right.

event that routinely attracts top anglers. The tournament was held on the Missouri River below the Oahe Dam, one of the premier walleye spots in the country.

A few days before the tournament, a blizzard pelted the area with 15 inches of heavy, wet snow. Then the weather warmed up rapidly and meltwater flooded the tributaries. By tournament time, the Missouri was running bankfull and the water resembled heavily creamed coffee.

One contestant phoned his wife after the first day with

this report, "Honey—I've got good news and bad news. The bad news is we didn't catch any fish today. The good news is we're tied for first place."

Amazingly, the story remained the same on the second day of the tournament. Ninety-three two-man teams failed to catch a single fish in the two-day event. The tournament sponsors refunded the entry fees.

So next time the walleyes get the best of you, don't bother checking your excuse cap—walleyes can humble even the top guns.

DEBUGGING YOUR WALLEYE PROGRAM

Ask a seasoned walleye pro to name the toughest walleye-fishing conditions, and I'll lay odds that "bug hatches" get mentioned early in the conversation.

Insects make up a relatively small percentage of a walleye's annual diet but, when a heavy hatch is in progress, they feed on insects almost exclusively. And as

many a frustrated angler will attest, walleyes are indifferent to any other food item once they go into insect-feeding mode.

Of all the insects walleyes consume, burrowing mayflies have the greatest impact on fishing. They hatch in tremendous quantities, and their large size means a walleye can eat its fill in a hurry.

"Mayflies make ideal fish food," says Dr. Calvin Fremling, one of the country's leading mayfly authorities. "The nymphs are super-abundant and they swim with an enticing wiggle that fish can't resist. They're also easy for the fish to catch and digest."

Burrowing mayfly nymphs, as their name suggests, dig

Walleyes literally gorge themselves on mayfly nymphs during a heavy hatch.

burrows in mud-silt-clay bottoms. The clay helps the burrows hold their form; a loose, silty bottom cannot support burrowing mayflies. Researchers have found mayfly nymphs at densities as heavy as 500 per square foot of bottom.

Massive hatches of burrowing mayflies, commonly called "fish flies," occur in many natural lakes and big rivers. The insects cover buildings, blanket parked cars and sometimes pile up so thick on roads and bridges that they create a traffic hazard.

Unless you've witnessed a major mayfly hatch, it's hard to imagine what it's like, but this report in an Iowa newspaper is quite descriptive: "Fish flies controlled the Julian Dubuque Bridge here for 40 minutes, then surrendered with heavy losses under an armored counter attack by highway commission scraper-trucks. Traffic was stopped on both sides of the Mississippi River bridge ..."

Hexagenia limbata, the common yellow mayfly found mainly in lakes, begins to hatch when the water reaches 53 degrees. The hatch peaks when the water warms to the low 70s.

Hexagenia bilineata, the most common big-river mayfly, hatches later than Hexagenia limbata. The hatch begins at 66 degrees and peaks at about 75.

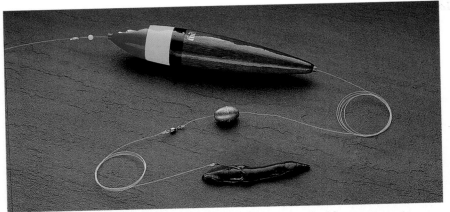

Make a slip-bobber rig for night-fishing by tying a bobber stop onto your line and threading on a bead, a good-sized bobber and a ½-ounce egg sinker. Then tie on a barrel swivel, an 18-inch leader and a size 6 bait hook. Select a lively leech and hook it through the middle of the body.

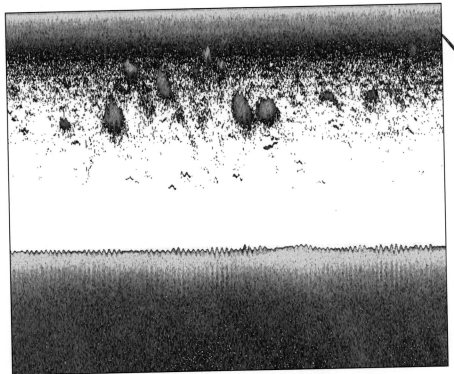

Use your sonar to spot mayfly-eating walleyes. The fish are easy to see because they're feeding well off the bottom. When the hatch is heavy, however, spotting the fish is more difficult because the nymphs obscure the walleyes.

Such massive hatches seldom occur in eutrophic lakes or polluted rivers, however, because their bottom muds do not contain adequate dissolved oxygen.

Most anglers believe that walleyes feed on adult mayflies, but that's not normally the case. While they may pick off a few adults, they're feeding mainly on nymphs as they emerge from their burrows and start to wiggle their way toward the surface.

The hatch usually begins in late afternoon and peaks before midnight, although some hatching continues until dawn. The heavier the hatch, the more actively the walleyes feed.

If you're fishing on the day after a major hatch, however, you'll be lucky to scrape up enough walleyes for a fish sandwich.

When the word gets out that a major insect hatch is in progress, most walleye anglers think they know how to solve the problem—stay home. But that's a big mistake, because the fish are highly catchable—you just have to be in the right place at the right time with the right presentation. Here are some strategies:

Night Fishing

"People think you can't catch walleyes during the mayfly hatch," says Terry Thurmer, proprietor of Terry's Boat Harbor on Minnesota's Mille Lacs Lake, "but as far as I'm concerned, it's the best time to catch them. In fact, I catch more 10-pound-plus walleyes during the mayfly hatch than at any other time of the year."

Thurmer, who is known as one of the big lake's top night-fishing guides, waits until the sun goes down and then motors his launch (party-boat) several miles out into the lake, parking it over known mayfly beds. "Most people think they have to fish the edges of the mud flats (mid-lake rises) where the bottom is firm. But that's not where the walleyes are when the hatch is on," Thurmer explains. "I'm fishing maybe a hundred yards off the flat, where the bottom is soft mud."

Thurmer relies on his sonar to pinpoint the walleyes. "They're easy to find," he says, "but most people

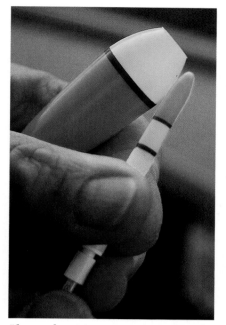

If your boat is not equipped with floodlights, use a lighted bobber powered by a tiny lithium battery.

How to Work a Mayfly Bed

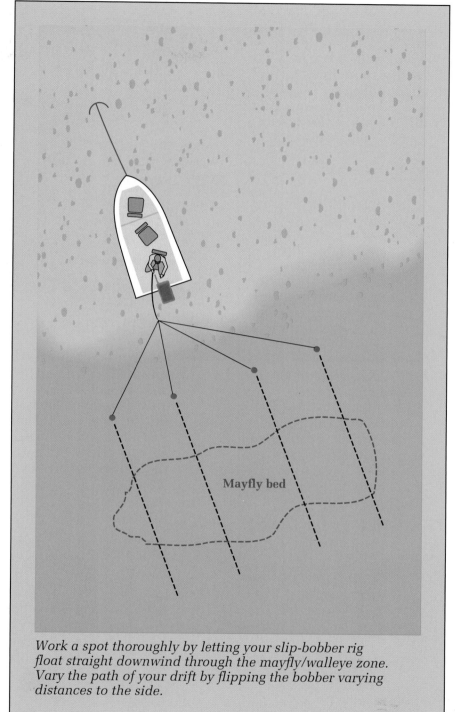

Work a spot thoroughly by letting your slip-bobber rig float straight downwind through the mayfly/walleye zone. Vary the path of your drift by flipping the bobber varying distances to the side.

don't try looting out in the middle of nowhere."

Once you find a walleye school, the rest is easy. Just toss out a lively leech on a slip-float rig set to fish 2 to 4 feet off bottom. When the fish start to feed, usually between 9pm and midnight, you won't have to wait long.

Why a slip-bobber rig? When mayfly nymphs emerge from the mud, they're an easy target. As they slowly wiggle their way to the surface, walleyes can pick them off at their leisure. Consequently, they go into a lazy feeding mode and refuse to chase bait.

Some anglers make the mistake of using a small slip-bobber and a light weight, assuming that the walleyes will be hitting softly. "I like a big float and a half-ounce sinker," says Thurmer. "It gets the bait down fast, so you're not wasting time when the fish are biting. And a big float is easy to see at night."

Thurmer's launch is equipped with strong halogen floodlights, so seeing the bobber is no problem. But if you don't have lights, you'll have to rely on a lighted bobber.

If you're lucky enough to find an active mayfly bed, be sure to punch its location into your GPS or establish a visual landmark. The fish will hang around the area even when there is no major hatch in progress. In fact, mayfly beds make some of the very best ice-fishing spots, not only for walleyes but also for jumbo perch.

Daytime Methods

If you're not a night stalker, plan on working a lot harder for your walleyes. When a hatch is on, they feed only sporadically in daylight hours.

A slip-bobber presentation is still the best choice, but a few additional refinements are necessary to tempt the super-finicky fish:

- Use smaller leeches (no more than 2 inches long). They work much better than "jumbos," probably because they're closer in size to a mayfly nymph and have a similar wiggling action. If you don't have small leeches, try half a 'crawler.
- Hook the leech on a ⅟₁₆-ounce jig head. The jig head is not so much for attraction as for restricting the movement of the leech so a walleye doesn't have to chase it.

Lures for Fishing Bug Hatches

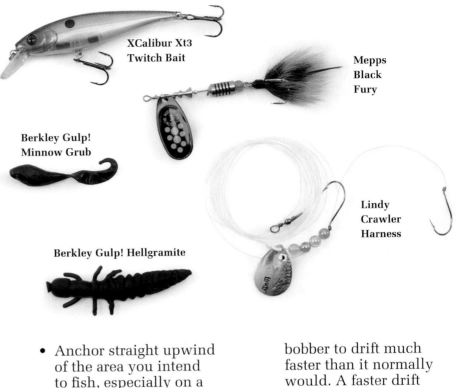

XCalibur Xt3
Twitch Bait

Mepps
Black
Fury

Berkley Gulp!
Minnow Grub

Lindy
Crawler
Harness

Berkley Gulp! Hellgramite

- Anchor straight upwind of the area you intend to fish, especially on a windy day. If you anchor off to the side, you'll have to cast crosswind to reach your spot. The wind and waves will put a big bow in your line, causing your bobber to drift much faster than it normally would. A faster drift may be advantageous when the fish are active, but when they're in the insect-feeding mode, you want the slowest presentation possible.

Live Bait Rigs for Daytime Fishing

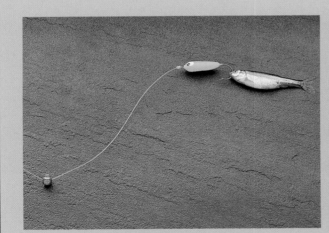

Make a split-shot rig by pinching on one or two split shot and then adding a floater tipped with a small minnow or leech.

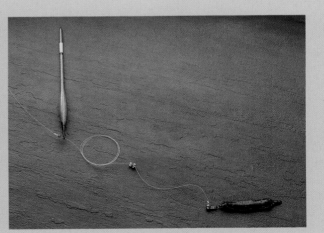

For daytime slip-bobber fishing, tie on a bobber stop and then thread on a bead and a slip-bobber. Add enough split shot to balance the float and attach a ⅟₁₆-ounce jig tipped with a small leech.

Burrowing Mayfly Life Cycle

Mayfly nymphs emerge from their burrows and migrate to the surface at night. When they reach the surface, they split their shells (exuviae) and crawl out of them in a minute or less. The newly emerged form, called a subamigo or dun, has cloudy wings and a grayish body.

The next afternoon, the dun undergoes a molt, shedding its skin and becoming an adult, or imago. The wings are now transparent and the body has a brownish or yellowish color.

The adults rest on trees and buildings during the day, but begin swarming at dusk. A male approaches a female from below, extends his legs upward to grasp her thorax, then begins in-flight copulation by turning his abdomen up to meet hers.

Females deposit their eggs, which may number over 8,000, on the water's surface. The eggs sink and adhere to the soft mud bottom; they hatch in two to three weeks. Within 30 hours of molting, most of the adults are dead.

The nymph constructs a "U" shaped burrow, resting in one arm of the burrow and facing upward. It feeds on organic matter in the mud. The nymphal stage lasts one to two years, depending on the species.

Nymph

Dun

Adult

A strong wind causes other problems too. When your bobber is bouncing up and down in big waves, you're vertically jigging without even trying, and that's not the way to catch insect feeders.

Some anglers prefer to nix the bobber and just cast with a ¹⁄₁₆-ounce jig tipped with a small leech or a dark-colored curlytail or tubebait. Using an ultralight spinning outfit spooled with 4-pound mono, inch the jig in as slowly as possible, resisting the urge to twitch it. Or, use a split-shot rig with a small leech or minnow on a plain hook, or a floater that will keep the bait off bottom (opposite).

If you see walleyes sipping adult mayflies off the surface, try a small suspending minnowbait. Cast well past the area where the fish are feeding and retrieve very slowly, pausing periodically to let the bait hang in the walleyes' faces. I've also had some success catching surface feeders on small in-line spinners.

Another obvious tactic for these insect feeders is fly fishing. Wait until the hatch is on, then toss out a mayfly-nymph pattern.

I've got a fly-fishing friend who looks forward to the bug hatches. "It's the best time for a fly fisherman to get a crack at walleyes," he says.

If you're not into night fishing or finessing the fish during daylight hours, the best solution is to try another lake where the bugs aren't hatching. Or, if you're fishing a lake with both mesotrophic and eutrophic basins, concentrate on the eutrophic portion; it probably won't have a significant mayfly hatch. Another thing to remember: The hatch may take place a week or two later on a deeper lake, and it could be that much earlier on a shallower one.

If you're a serious walleye angler, you're going to run up against a bug hatch sooner or later. So you've got a choice: spend your time commiserating with other anglers about the lousy fishing, or try the techniques we've described and get in on some of the year's fastest action.

THE FALL WALLEYE PUZZLE

The two phone calls came within a few hours of each other. The first one was from a friend who had been fishing on a large, shallow lake. "The walleyes are really slammin'," he reported. "Gettin' 'em in three feet of water."

The second call came from another friend on a deep, clear lake. "Caught an easy limit this morning," he said. "They all came out of 35 to 50 feet of water."

These two lakes are less than 60 miles apart, yet their fall walleye patterns bear no similarity. And therein lies the problem with fall walleye fishing; unless you have some inside information, you never really know where to start looking for the fish. Here, we'll help you understand why fall walleye patterns differ so greatly from lake to

lake, so you'll have a better idea of where to find the fish. Then, we'll show you the most effective techniques for catching them.

Why Fall Walleye Patterns Differ

To make any sense of fall walleye movements, it helps to understand the fall turnover (p.150). The turnover thoroughly mixes the water, removing any temperature or oxygen barriers that may have prevented fish from moving vertically in the summer. And with those barriers gone, the fish can go wherever food is most abundant.

Fall walleyes are most likely to be shallow in big, windswept lakes with shallow, relatively featureless

basins and water of low to moderate clarity—like the lake my first friend had called about. Most lakes of this type have tremendous populations of baitfish—most commonly yellow perch.

Huge numbers of young-of-the-year perch congregate in the shallows beginning in late summer and continuing well into the fall. They move in to feed on plankton, which is pushed shoreward by the wind. Walleyes, in turn, move in to feed on the perch. Because the windswept shallows are nearly devoid of aquatic vegetation, the perch can freely move about to graze on plankton, and the walleyes can easily move about to feed on the perch. The pattern is similar with shiners and most other common baitfish species.

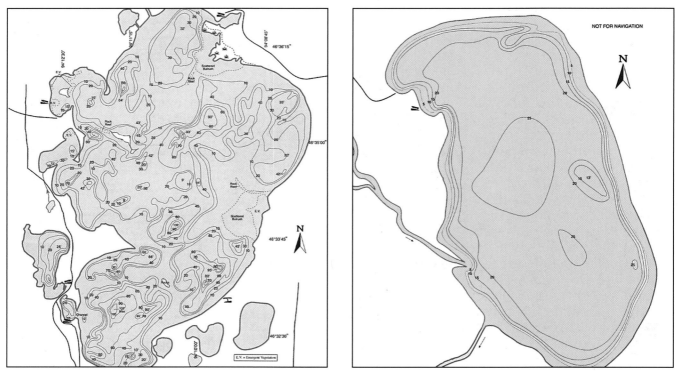

Fall walleye patterns differ greatly depending mainly on depth and water clarity. The fish are usually deeper in a deep, clear lake (left) than in a shallow, discolored lake (right).

Understanding The Fall Turnover

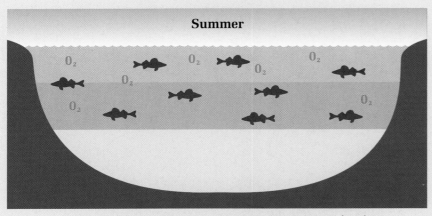

Summer

During summer, most lakes stratify into three layers: the epilimnion (pink), the metalimnion (purple) and the hypolimnion (blue). Walleyes are usually found in the upper two layers; the deep water may not have sufficient oxygen.

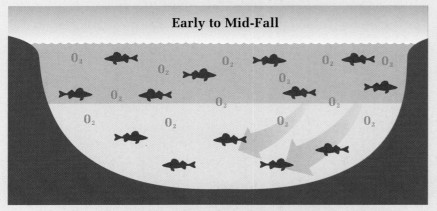

Early to Mid-Fall

In early to mid-fall, the surface water begins to cool and sink. When the shallows reach the same temperature as the depths, wind causes the entire lake to circulate, evening out the water temperature and oxygen level. Walleyes may be found at any depth.

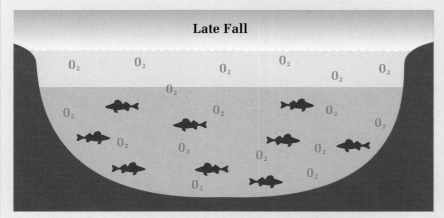

Late Fall

By late fall, the water is warmest near the bottom, so most of the walleyes have moved deep. In shallow lakes, however, the wind may keep the lake turning over almost until freeze-up, so the fish are scattered, just as they were earlier in the turnover period.

What is the Fall Turnover?

The fall turnover is the period of time, usually in early to mid-fall, when the lake is circulating from top to bottom and the water temperature is uniform throughout.

Turnover Basics

In summer, most natural lakes stratify into three distinct temperature layers: the upper layer, or epilimnion; the middle layer, or metalimnion; and the lower layer, or *hypolimnion*.

Water in the epilimnion is warmer and thus lighter than that in the metalimnion and, as a result of the density difference, is easily circulated by the wind. Any water below the epilimnion resists mixing. As a result, the epilimnion stays uniformly warm and well oxygenated, while the temperature and oxygen level drops through the metalimnion. The part of the metalimnion where the temperature drops fastest is called the *thermocline*. The hypolimnion has the coldest water and lowest oxygen level.

Because of this stratification, the walleye's vertical feeding movements are restricted by temperature and/or oxygen barriers. In most lakes, you'll find the greatest number of summer walleyes in the middle to lower part of the metalimnion, usually at depths of 15 to 25 feet. They may make short feeding runs into the shallows, but they won't tolerate the warm temperatures for long.

As the surface water begins to cool in early fall, it gets denser than the warmer water below, causing it to sink. The surface water keeps cooling and sinking until the entire lake is the same temperature from top to bottom. Then, with the density of the water now equalized, even a light wind causes all of the water in the lake to mix. With all temperature or oxygen barriers to vertical movement now removed, walleyes may again be found at any depth.

The turnover may occur at different times, even on adjacent lakes, depending on the shape of the lake basin. All other factors being equal, a deep lake turns over later than a shallow one. The depths are much colder in a deep lake, and it takes longer for the surface water to cool enough to match the temperature in the depths.

In late fall, the temperature in the depths is usually a little warmer than that in the shallows. Water is densest at a temperature of 39.2 degrees. When it cools below that point, it becomes less dense, so it does not sink. This explains why lakes do not freeze to the bottom.

Recognizing Turnover

The sure way to determine if a lake is turning over is to check the temperature with an electric thermometer. Find the deepest part of the lake and lower the probe to the bottom. If the turnover is in progress, the entire water column should be at the same temperature, give or take a degree or two.

An electric thermometer gives you the water temperature at any depth.

If you don't have an electric thermometer, here are some clues that will give you a pretty good idea of what's going on below:

- A sudden decrease in water clarity is a pretty good indication that the turnover has started. Water circulation puts fine particles of silt and clay into suspension, explaining why the water often looks cloudy.
- Circulating water also causes clumps of decaying organic matter to break loose from the bottom and float to the surface. Sometimes you'll see large mats of brownish glop floating everywhere.
- If you run a sensitive graph over deep water, you'll see small baitfish scattered at all depths.

Some fishermen even claim they notice a different odor to the water when a lake starts to turn over.

How Turnover Affects Fishing

Because the turnover evens out the water temperature and restores oxygen to the depths, it opens up fish habitat that was not previously available. In most lakes, low oxygen levels prevent the fish from going deep in summer, so they're confined to a relatively narrow depth range. During the turnover, however, the fish can be at practically any depth. With so much more water to search, your odds of finding them are greatly reduced.

Most anglers seem to think that turnover lasts only a few days and, once it's over, fishing gets back to normal. But according to Dr. Robert Megard, a prominent limnology professor, that is definitely not the case. "The turnover lasts as long as the lake is cooling," Megard points out. "As the density of the surface water increases, it sinks, creating density plumes or thermals that can be detected with sonar. For all practical purposes, turnover continues until freeze-up."

But the turnover doesn't necessarily mean bad fishing. In fact, most gamefish species are concentrated more tightly during the turnover period than at any other time of the year. This explains why fall fishing is so "spot" oriented.

In summer, you'll find fish scattered over large flats, cruising the weedlines or even chasing baitfish in open water. But in fall, clumps of fish hold in very precise locations. They could be on the end of a tiny rock pile, in a sharp inside turn along a breakline or tucked into a small patch of green weeds. Most fish use sharp-breaking structure in fall, so even if they're resting in deep water and feeding in much shallower water, they're not moving far. If you can locate one of these fall hotspots, you'll enjoy some of the year's fastest action.

It pays to spend some extra time studying your sonar during the turnover. Cruise around and check out every nook and cranny of a particular piece of structure. If you aren't super-meticulous in your coverage, you could easily miss a tight school, meaning the difference between a bad day and a terrific one.

Once the fish set up in their late fall locations, they're likely to stay there until freeze-up and possibly well into the winter season. Should you find one of these tight schools, get a good landmark on the spot or punch it into your GPS. Chances are the fish will be right there next time you come back.

What's also confusing is that the fall pattern on a murky lake may be completely different than that on a clear one, even if the two are similar in depth. Fish in low-clarity lakes are not likely to go deep at turnover time, probably because they cannot see well enough to feed in the murky water. In clear lakes, however, there is practically no limit to how deep the fish will go.

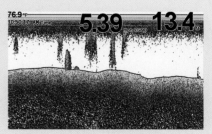

When you see baitfish scattered at all depths, the lake is probably turning over.

Fall walleyes are most likely to be deep in smaller, highly structured lakes with deep, clear water. Perch may be common in these lakes, but their density does not compare to that in larger, shallower, more windswept waters.

The shallows of these deeper lakes often hold fair numbers of perch, but many areas are so choked with weeds that walleyes would have trouble maneuvering well enough to catch them. Besides, the high water clarity is not conducive to shallow-water feeding. In the clear water, weeds often grow to a depth of 25 feet and, after the lake stratifies, walleyes normally feed in the 25- to 30-foot depth range. If they went deeper, they would find cold water with few, if any, baitfish of any kind. But in fall, with the temperature barrier removed, the perch go even deeper and so do the walleyes. I've caught them as deep as 55 feet.

But there's a twist to the typical fall walleye pattern in these clear lakes. After dark, the fish move out of the depths and begin cruising shallow shoal areas. I've found them as shallow as three feet, but more typically, they'll be at depths of eight to 12. You may find them on a clean rocky or gravelly bottom but, more often, they cruise over weedbeds, picking off small perch or other baitfish that have moved out of the dense weeds to feed on plankton and invertebrates.

Here's yet another complication to the fall walleye puzzle: If a lake has one deep, clear basin and another basin with shallower, darker water, it may have deep-water and shallow-water walleye patterns occurring simultaneously.

Tactics for Fall Walleyes

The first and most obvious step in solving the fall walleye puzzle is determining whether the lake you're fishing has a deep-water pattern, a shallow-water pattern, or both. The lake-type guidelines provided earlier will

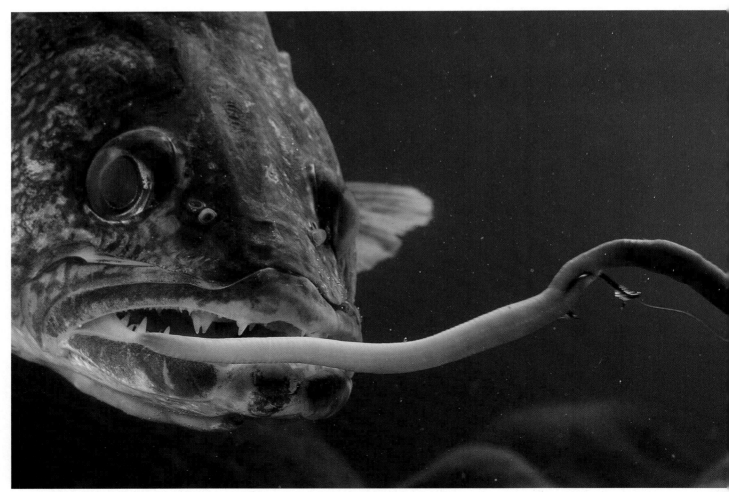

A spinner blade can make a big difference when there is a glut of baitfish.

go a long way in helping you make that determination. But sometimes the walleyes will fool you. If you're fishing an unfamiliar lake, do a little research before you start. Hang around the boat landing and chat with anglers coming and going to see what you can learn. Very few fishermen will divulge their spots, but most are willing to tell you the best fishing times and the most productive depths. You may also pick up some information from the local bait-shop operator, fisheries manager or game warden.

Shallow-Water Patterns

When clouds of young-of-the-year baitfish overrun the shallows in early fall, walleyes

can eat their fill in minutes, making them tough to catch. One way to trigger a reaction from these stubborn walleyes is to add a Colorado spinner blade ahead of the hook. The added flash and vibration can double or triple the number of strikes. Experiment with size and color of the blade. I normally use a size 4 or 5 blade, in silver or gold. But in low-clarity water, a fluorescent-colored blade is a better choice. Be sure to use a Colorado-style blade, because it will turn at a very slow trolling speed.

Another good triggering technique is rip-jigging (p.91) along shallow, gradually sloping breaklines.

When walleyes move into shallow water at night, try some longline trolling with floating minnowbaits. I prefer silver or perch-pattern floating Rapalas in sizes 11 or 13. There is no need to get them down to the bottom; in fact, you'll do much better by keeping them a few feet above it. Night-feeding walleyes are accustomed to looking up for their food, spotting its silhouette against the moonlit or starlit sky. You can make the bait track a

Lighted markers (arrow) allow precision trolling.

little deeper by adding split shot or a small twist-on sinker. If the wind was blowing during the day, do your nighttime trolling along the windward shore; that's where the walleyes are most likely to be.

Shallow rocky reefs are also good night-trolling spots in fall. But to ensure that you're trolling in the right area, place lighted markers along your trolling route.

Should you catch a couple of fish in the same area, stop trolling and work the spot thoroughly by casting. There may be a slight indentation in the breakline, a patch of weeds or gravel or some other feature that is concentrating the fish.

Making a Spinner Rig

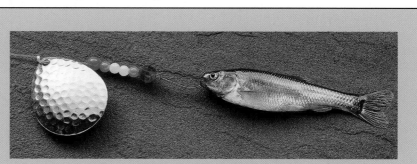

Make your own spinner rig by threading a size 5 or 6 Colorado blade into a clevis and then threading the clevis onto your line so the convex side of the blade is facing forward as the rig is pulled ahead. Then thread on several colored beads and tie on a bait hook.

Here's a little trick that will give your minnow-bait a more enticing action and also make it run a tad deeper. Tie the bait directly to 6- or 8-pound mono, using a Trilene or Palomar knot. Cinch the knot tightly, then position it on the lower part of the eye, rather than right on the end. This way, the line pulls the nose slightly downward, giving the bait considerably more wobble. When you hook a fish or a snag, the knot will slide back up the eye and you'll have to pull it back down again.

Slide your knot to the lower portion of the eye for maximum wiggle.

Deep-Water Patterns

Because walleyes make such extreme vertical movements in fall, they prefer sharp drop-offs to gradual ones. This way, they can feed in the shallows at night, then easily slip out to deep water to spend the day. Fall schools tend to be very tight; sometimes you'll find a knot of walleyes tucked into a tiny notch in the breakline and no fish for hundreds of yards on either side.

Fishing such specific structure requires precise boat control. Use a high-thrust electric trolling motor to hold directly over the spot while working it with live bait on either a slip-sinker rig or a jig. It's of vital importance to keep your line as vertical as possible. If you don't use enough weight, your line will trail off at too much of an angle, and you won't be able to keep your bait in the fish zone. Nor will you be able to detect strikes or get solid hooksets. For slip-sinker fishing, you'll need a ½- to ¾-ounce sinker; for jig fishing, a ⅜- to ½-ounce leadhead.

I rely heavily on minnows for fall fishing, especially late in the season, but there are times when a ribbon leech or nightcrawler works better. It's hard to know for sure what will work best, so I usually carry all three.

My favorite fall minnow is the redtail chub, which is one of the largest walleye baits. Bigger baits work well in fall, because the natural forage has grown considerably larger over the summer. I normally use redtails from 4 to 5 inches long, but for trophy-class walleyes, I may even go with 6-inchers. Redtails work better than other large walleye baits like suckers and

A jig tipped with a redtail chub is a top fall walleye bait.

big shiners, because they're much tougher. If you tip a jig with a sucker, for instance, it will probably be dead after a few casts.

Because redtails are so tough, you have the option of hooking them in the tail (p.82), which makes them struggle extra hard and draw the walleyes' attention.

Sure, figuring out fall walleye patterns can be a big challenge. But there's also a big payoff. Fall is one of the best times of the year to catch big walleyes, because the females are feeding heavily to nourish their developing eggs. And with much of the competition out hunting or home huddled around the fire, you'll probably have the entire lake to yourself.

Finding Fall Walleyes in Deep Lakes

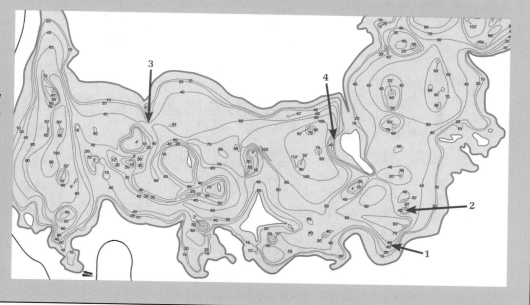

Typical fall walleye hotspots in deep lakes include (1) a sharp inside turn on a deep breakline, (2) a deep hump, (3) a sharp-sloping lip of an extended point and (4) a steep area along the breakline.

To Fizz or Not to Fizz?

If you've ever caught a walleye in water more than 30 feet deep and attempted to release it, you know the problem. Instead of swimming back to the bottom, the fish struggles upside down on the surface, unable to right itself.

What has happened is that its swim bladder has expanded because of the change in water pressure between the bottom and the surface. In some cases, the swim bladder expands so much that it forces the fish's stomach out its mouth.

In an attempt to save these fish, tournament anglers and other fishermen have experimented with a technique called "fizzing." By inserting a hypodermic needle through the side or belly and into the swim bladder, the excess gas is released (making a fizzing sound) and the fish can hopefully right itself and swim away.

But research recently conducted in Alberta found that fizzing did

The practice of "fizzing," or deflating the swim bladder with a hypodermic needle, has not proven beneficial.

not increase walleye survival and, in some cases, survival of fizzed walleyes was lower than that of unfizzed fish. Here is a summary of the study results:

- Biologists found 100 percent survival among fizzed and unfizzed walleyes caught at depths of less than 20 feet.
- The survival rate was 88 to 94 percent for both fizzed and unfizzed fish taken from depths of 20 to 25 feet.

- The survival rate for unfizzed walleyes taken from depths of 25 to 33 feet was 89 to 90 percent. The survival rate of fizzed walleyes taken from those depths was 42 to 66 percent.

Instead of increasing survival of walleyes taken in deep water, fizzing significantly decreased it.

Subsequent tests showed deep-caught walleyes had other physiological problems in addition to an over-inflated swim bladder. The electrolyte and protein balance of their blood was off kilter, and they showed signs of muscle injury and insufficient oxygen levels in the blood.

Fish that had been fizzed exhibited additional signs of stress as reflected by a reduction in certain types of blood cells.

So if you plan on releasing deep-caught walleyes, get them back into the water as fast as you can and don't attempt to fizz them.

INDEX